Διαβάστε και μιλήστε Ελληνικά

READ and SPEAK

GREEK

Language Pack for Beginners

by Hara Garoufalia
Howard Middle

Published by g-and-w PUBLISHING
47a High Street
Chinnor
Oxfordshire OX39 4DJ

First published 2008

© g-and-w PUBLISHING 2008

ISBN 13: 978-1-903103-21-0

ISBN 10: 1-903103-21-5

Designed by: Mark Wightwick

Illustrated by: Leila Gaafar

Printed in China
by Wing King Tong Co. Ltd.

1 2 3 4 5 6 7 8 9   15 14 13 12 11 10 09 08

CONTENTS

4   Introduction

5   **TOPIC 1:** What's your name?

⊙ Basic greetings

⊙ Saying and asking about names

14   **TOPIC 2:** Where are you from?

⊙ Countries

⊙ Saying where you're from

24   **TOPIC 3:** What's this?

⊙ Asking about what things are

⊙ Ordering drinks and snacks

34   **TOPIC 4:** Where is it?

⊙ Describing where things are

⊙ Expressing negatives

44   **TOPIC 5:** What's it like?

⊙ Describing characteristics

⊙ Adjectives

54   **TOPIC 6:** How do I get there?

⊙ Places around town

⊙ Transportation

⊙ Directions and instructions

64   **TOPIC 7:** Who's this?

⊙ Describing your family

⊙ Possessives (*my, your*, etc.)

⊙ Numbers 1–10

74   **TOPIC 8:** What do you do?

⊙ Describing occupations

⊙ Talking about where you work

84   Test Yourself

89   Reference

92   Answer Key

✴ *plus...*

8 tear-out cards for fun games

Audio CD to enhance your learning

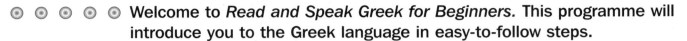

INTRODUCTION

○ ○ ○ ○ ○ Welcome to *Read and Speak Greek for Beginners.* This programme will introduce you to the Greek language in easy-to-follow steps.

○ ○ ○ ○ The focus is on enjoyment and understanding, on *reading* words rather than writing them yourself. Through activities and games you'll learn how to read and speak basic Greek in less time than you thought possible.

○ ○ ○ You'll find these features in your programme:

Key Words	see them written and hear them on the CD to improve your pronunciation
Language Focuses	clear, simple explanations of language points to help you build up phrases for yourself
Activities	practice what you have learned in reading, listening, and speaking activities
Games	with tear-out components. Challenge yourself or play with a friend. A great, fun way to review
Audio CD	hear the key words and phrases and take part in interactive listening and speaking activities. You'll find the track numbers next to the activities in your book

○ ○ If you want to give yourself extra confidence with reading the script, you will find *Your First 100 Words in Greek* the ideal pre-course companion to this programme. *Your First 100 Words in Greek* introduces the Greek script through 100 key everyday words, many of which also feature in *Read and Speak Greek for Beginners.*

○ So now you can take your first steps in Greek with confidence, enjoyment, and a real sense of progress.

○ *Whenever you see the audio CD symbol, you'll find listening and*
○ *speaking activities on the CD included with this book. The symbol*
○ *shows the track number.*
○
○ *Track 1 is an introduction to the sounds of Greek.*
○ *Listen to this before you start and come back to it again at*
○ *later stages if you need to.*
○

Key Words

Look at the script for each key word and try to visualize it, connecting its image to the pronunciation you hear on your CD.

γειά σας **yiá sas**   *hello* (polite)

γειά σου **yiá soo**   *hello* (informal)

αντίο **adío**   *goodbye*

το όνομά μου είναι...
to ónomá moo íne...   *my name is...*

Greek names:

Μαρία **maría** (female)

Άννα **ánna** (female)

Κώστας **kóstas** (male)

Γιώργος **yiórgos** (male)

TRACK NUMBER
2

The Greek alphabet has 24 characters. Many look and are pronounced similar to the English (Roman) alphabet; some look familiar but are pronounced differently; and some look and sound completely different. In general, Greek words can be pronounced exactly as they are written – unlike some English sounds such as "ough" as in rough, cough, through, though, *etc. which all look the same but are pronounced differently.*

Refer to the alphabet table on page 90 if you want to work out the individual letters in a word, but try to recognize the general shape of the words in Greek as you go along.

TOPIC 1: What's your name?

How do you say it?

Join the script to the pronunciation, as in the example.

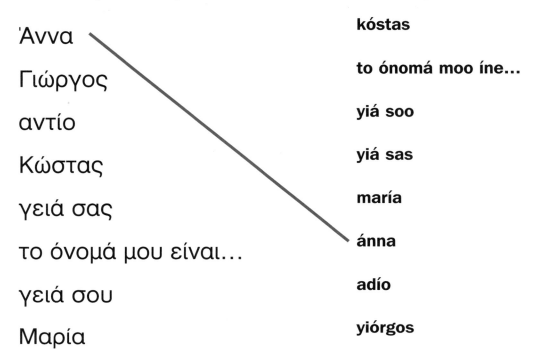

Άννα   kóstas

Γιώργος   to ónomá moo íne...

αντίο   yiá soo

Κώστας   yiá sas

γειά σας   maría

το όνομά μου είναι...   ánna

γειά σου   adío

Μαρία   yiórgos

What does it mean?

Now say the Greek out loud and write the English next to each.

γειά σας ___hello (polite)___   το όνομά μου είναι...

Κώστας _____   _____

Άννα _____   αντίο _____

γειά σου _____   Γιώργος _____

Μαρία _____

Language Focus

⊙ ⊙ ⊙ ⊙ In Greek, the word for "my" (or "your", "his", etc) comes after όνομά **ónomá** ("name"). "My name" is literally "the name my":

> Το όνομά μου είναι Άννα. **to ónomá moo íne ánna**
> *My name is Anna.*
>
> Το όνομά μου είναι Κώστας. **to ónomá moo íne kóstas** *My name is Kostas.*

⊙ ⊙ ⊙ ⊙ As with some other languages such as French, there are two ways in Greek of saying "you" or "your" – a polite way for people we don't know, and an informal way for friends, relatives and children. The polite way is also used when addressing more than one person (even if they are friends).

⊙ ⊙ ⊙ In Greek, γειά σας **yiá sas** means "your health", or literally "health your". The word σας **sas** is the polite way of saying "your" and is also used for more than one person. If you are only talking to one person you know well, use the informal word for "your", σου **soo**: γειά σου **yiá soo**.

> Γειά σας, κύριε Γιώργο. **yia sas, kírie yiórgo**
> *Hello, Mr Yiorgo.*
>
> Γειά σου, Μαρία. **yia soo, maría**
> *Hello, Maria.*

⊙ ⊙ Greek uses accent marks above vowels to show the stress, i.e. where you place the emphasis on a particular word. These marks will help you pronounce the words correctly.

TRACK NUMBER
3

⊙
⊙   *Practice introducing yourself and learn some*
⊙   *useful replies on your CD.*
⊙

⊙ ⊙

TOPIC 1: What's your name?

ACTIVITIES

What are they saying?

Write the correct number in the word balloons.

1 Γειά σου. Το όνομά μου
είναι Μαρία.
**yiá soo. to ónomá moo íne
maría**

2 Γειά σου, Γιώργο.
yiá soo, yiorgo

3 Αντίο. **adío**

4 Γειά σου, Άννα.
yiá soo, anna

What do you hear?

Work out the phrases below. Then listen and
tick (✔) the two phrases you hear on your
audio CD.

TRACK NUMBER
4

1 Αντίο, Άννα. ❑

2 Το όνομά μου είναι Κώστας. ❑

3 Αντίο, Γιώργο. ❑

4 Γειά σας, Μαρία. ❑

5 Γειά σας. ❑

TOPIC 1: What's your name?

Key Words

TRACK NUMBER
5

πώς είναι...; **pos íne...?**		*what is...?*
πώς είναι το όνομά σας; **pos íne to ónomá sas?**		*what is your name?* (polite/plural)
πώς είναι το όνομά σου; **pos íne to ónomá soo?**		*what is your name?* (informal)
παρακαλώ **parakaló**		*please*
ευχαριστώ **efharistó**		*thank you*
καλημέρα **kaliméra**		*good morning*
καλησπέρα **kálispéra**		*good evening*

Language Focus

⊚ ⊚ ⊚ ⊚ In the Greek script, a question mark looks like a semi-colon: Πώς; *What?*

⊚ ⊚ ⊚ ⊚ To form the question "What's your name?", the Greek follows the same pattern as in English: Πώς **pos** *what* + είναι **íne** *is* + το όνομά σας **to ónoma sas** *your name* (literally, "the name your").

⊚ ⊚ ⊚ If you are asking a child, you use the singular, informal word for "your", σου **soo**:

> Γειά σου. Πώς είναι το όνομά σου;
> **yia soo. pos íne to ónomá soo?**
> *Hello. What's your name?.*

Speaking practice

TRACK NUMBER
6

Practice the Greek you have learned so far.

What does it mean?

Match the English word balloons to the Greek.

For example: 1d

1 Good morning.

2 Hello.

3 What's your name?

4 Please.

5 My name's Maria.

6 Thank you.

a Παρακαλώ.

b Το όνομά μου είναι Μαρία.

c Ευχαριστώ.

d Καλημέρα.

e Πώς είναι το όνομά σας;

f Γειά σας.

Which word?

Write the correct number of the word in the box to complete the conversation, as in the example.

1 μου	2 σπέρα	3 σας
4 όνομά	5 καλη	6 είναι

Καλη_____ .

Γειά σας, _____σπέρα.

Το _____ μου _____ Άννα.

Πως είναι το όνομά _____ ;

Το όνομά _____ είναι Γιώργος.

TOPIC 1: What's your name?

Language Focus

◎ ◎ ◎ ◎ To say "Mr" and "Mrs" in Greek, we use κύριος **kírios** (*Mr*) and κυρία **kiría** (*Mrs*). Notice that the stress changes. These words can be used with the first name or surname. There is no Greek equivalent of "Ms".

◎ ◎ ◎ ◎ When you speak to a man and use the word for Mr, it changes from κύριος **kírios** to κύριε **kírie**. In addition, the final ς **-s** is deleted from the name.

> καλημέρα, κύριε Γιώργο.
>
> **kaliméra, kírie yiórgo**
>
> *Good morning, Mr Yiorgo.*

What are their names?

Can you work out these common English names in Greek script?
Use the alphabet tables on page 90–91 to help you work them out.

Κάθριν	_Catherine_	Τζων	_____
Μαίρη	_____	Ντέϊβιντ	_____
Άνν	_____	Μάϊκλ	_____
Ελίζαμπεθ	_____	Χάρρυ	_____

In or out?

Who is in the office today and who is out at meetings? Look at the wallchart and write the names in English in the correct column, as in the example.

Ελίζαμπεθ	✔
Τζων	✔
Άννα	✘
Χάρρυ	✔
Κώστας	✘
Μάϊκλ	✘
Κάθριν	✔
Ντέϊβιντ	✔
Γιώργος	✘
Μαίρη	✘

IN

Elizabeth

OUT

The Name Game

1 Tear out Game Card 1 at the back of your book and cut out the name cards (leave the sentence-build cards at the bottom of the sheet for the moment).

2 Put the cards Greek side up and see if you can recognize the names. Turn over the cards to see if you were correct.

3 Keep shuffling the cards and testing yourself until you can read all the names.

4 Then cut out the extra sentence-build cards at the bottom of the sheet and make mini-dialogues. For example:

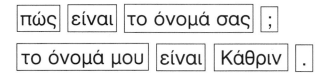

– pos íne to ónomá sas?

– to ónomá moo íne káthrin

5 You can also play with a friend. Make mini-dialogues for each other to read. If you both have a book, you can play pairs (pelmanism) with both sets of cards, saying the words as you turn over the cards.

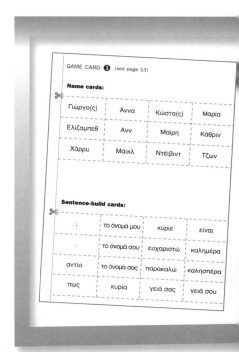

GAME CARD ❶ (see page 13)

Name cards:

Γιώργο(ς)	Άννα	Κώστα(ς)	Μαρία
Ελίζαμπεθ	Άνν	Μαίρη	Κάθριν
Χάρρυ	Μάικλ	Ντέιβιντ	Τζων

Sentence-build cards:

;	το όνομά μου	κύριε	είναι
.	το όνομά σου	ευχαριστώ	καλημέρα
αντίο	το όνομά σας	παρακαλώ	καλησπέρα
πώς	κυρία	γειά σας	γειά σου

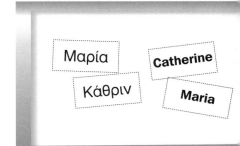

TOPIC 1: What's your name?

Key Words

TRACK NUMBER
7

η Ελλάδα **i elláтha**	Greece	ο Καναδάς **o kanathás**	Canada
η Ιταλία **i italía**	Italy	η Ιρλανδία **i irlanтhía**	Ireland
η Τουρκία **i tourkía**	Turkey	η Αυστραλία **i avstralía**	Australia
η Αγγλία **i anglía**	England	
η Αμερική **i amerikí**	America	η πόλη **i póli**	city
		η χώρα **i hóra**	country

*When you are talking about a country or city in Greek, the word for "the" has to be included before the name. Also, you'll see that the form of the word for "the" is not always the same. That is because in Greek there are three genders for all objects, names, places, etc.: masculine, feminine and neuter (see page 27 for more details). Most countries are feminine, so the word for "the" is η **i**. However, Canada is masculine, and has ο **o** for "the". The neuter word for "the" is το **to**. There are very few countries that have the neuter gender, but several <u>cities</u> are neuter, for example: το Λονδίνο **to lonтhíno** London.*

*Notice that **тh** in the pronunciation guide indicates the sound is like the "th" in "<u>that</u>". Otherwise **th** is pronounced as in "<u>thin</u>".*

TOPIC 2: Where are you from?

Where are the countries?

Write the number next to the country, as in the example.

ο Καναδάς _1_   η Ελλάδα ___   η Αγγλία ___   η Ιταλία ___

η Ιρλανδία ___   η Αμερική ___   η Τουρκία ___   η Αυστραλία ___

TOPIC 2: Where are you from?

How do you say it?

Join the English to the pronunciation and the Greek script, as in the example.

English	Pronunciation	Greek
England	**i tourkía**	η χώρα
Turkey	**i amerikí**	η Αυστραλία
Ireland	**o kaнaтнás**	η Ελλάδα
city	**i ellátнa**	η Ιταλία
Italy	**i irlaнтнía**	η Αμερική
Canada	**i hóra**	ο Καναδάς
America	**i avstralía**	η Ιρλανδία
country	**i italía**	η Αγγλία
Australia	**i póli**	η Τουρκία
Greece	**i anglía**	η πόλη

Where are the cities?

Read the Language Focus on page 17 before you try this activity. Then look at these cities and make sentences about where they are as in the example.

Το Λονδίνο είναι στην Αγγλία. **to lonтнíno íne stin anglía** [The] London is in [the] England.

Athens	New York	Washington	Ankara
η Αθήνα	η Νέα Υόρκη	η Ουάσινγκτον	η Άγκυρα
i athína	**i nea yórki**	**i ouásington**	**i ángira**

Thessaloniki	Sydney	London	Dublin
η Θεσσαλονίκη	το Σίντνεϊ	το Λονδίνο	το Δουβλίνο
i thessaloníki	**to sídnei**	**to lonтнíno**	**to doovlíno**

TOPIC 2: Where are you from?

Language Focus

It is straightforward to say where you are from. Use the phrase Εγώ είμαι από... **egó íme apó...** *I am from...* and add the name of the country or town. The masculine and feminine words for "the" change from Ο **o** and η **i** to ΤΟΝ **ton** and ΤΗΝ **tin** after από **apó**. The neuter ΤΟ **to** stays the same.

> Εγώ είμαι από την Ελλάδα.
> **egó íme apó tin elláτΗα** *I am from [the] Greece.*
>
> Εγώ είμαι από τον Καναδά.
> **egó íme apo ton kanaτΗá** *I am from [the] Canada.*

To say *in*, we use σε **se**, which becomes simply σ **s** when you put it in front of την **tin**, τον **ton**, or το **to**: σε + την/τον/το = στην/στον/στο.

> Εγώ είμαι από την Ουάσινγκτον, στην Αμερική.
> **egó íme apo ton ouásington, stin amerikí**
> *I am from [the] Washington, in [the] America.*

To say *near*, we use the word κοντά **kontá** in front of the phrase for *"in the"*:

> Εγώ είμαι από την Οξφόρδη, μία πόλη
> κοντά στο Λονδίνο. **egó íme apo tin oksfórτΗi,**
> **mia póli kontá sto lonτΗíno**
> *I am from [the] Oxford, a city near [the] London.*

If you want to ask someone where they are from, you need to use the question Από πού είστε εσείς; **apo poo íste esís?** *From where are you?*

> Από πού είστε εσείς, Μαρία;
> **apo poo íste esís, maría?** *Where are you from, Maria?*

TRACK NUMBER
8

Listen to six different people introducing themselves and see if you can understand where they are from.

Where are they from?

Join the people to their nationalities, as in the example. Listen again to track 8 on your CD and look back at the names and countries if you need to remind yourself.

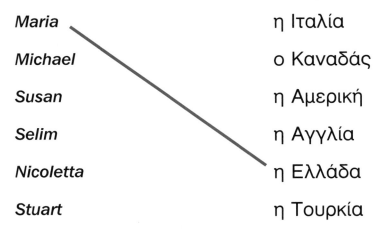

Maria	η Ιταλία
Michael	ο Καναδάς
Susan	η Αμερική
Selim	η Αγγλία
Nicoletta	η Ελλάδα
Stuart	η Τουρκία

Where are *you* from?

Now say where you're from.
Follow the prompts on your audio CD.

TRACK NUMBER
9

Key Words

TRACK NUMBER
10

εγώ είμαι **egó íme**	*I am*	αυτός είναι **aftós íne**	*he is*
εσείς είστε **esís íste**	*you are* (polite/plural)	αυτή είναι **aftí íne**	*she is*
		από **apó**	*from*
εσύ είσαι **esí íse**	*you are* (informal)	πού; **poo?**	*where?*

TOPIC 2: Where are you from?

Language Focus

◎ ◎ ◎ ◎ You now know how to ask and answer questions about where you're from:

> Από πού είστε; **apo poo íste?**
> *Where are you from?*
>
> Είμαι από την Ελλάδα. **íme apo tin ellá**тна
> *I am from Greece.*

◎ ◎ ◎ ◎ Notice that the question and answer above doesn't include the words for "I" (εγώ **egó**) or "you" (εσείς/εσύ **esís/esí**). In Greek we don't usually need to include these words as the form of the verb already tells us who is speaking.

◎ ◎ ◎ If you want to talk about where someone else is from, you use αυτός **aftós** (he) or αυτή **aftí** (she):

> Από πού είναι αυτός; **apó poo íne aftós?**
> *Where's he from?*
>
> Αυτός είναι από την Αμερική.
> **aftós íne apó tin amerikí**
> *He's from America.*
>
> Από πού είναι αυτή; **apó poo íne aftí?**
> *Where's she from?*
>
> Αυτή είναι από την Αθήνα, στην Ελλάδα.
> **aftí íne apó tin athína, stin elá**тна
> *She's from Athens, in Greece.*

◎ ◎ Remember that in Greek the word for "the" has to go in front of the city or country with the masculine and feminine words changing from Ο **o** and η **i**, to τον **ton** and την **tin** after a preposition like από **apó**. The neuter το **to** stays the same.

Who's from where?

Make questions and answers about where these people are from, as in the example.

Από πού είναι αυτός;
apó poo íne aftós?
Where's he from?

Αυτός είναι από την Νέα Υόρκη, στην Αμερική.
aftós íne apó tin Néa Yórki, stin Amerikí
He is from New York, in America.

TOPIC 2: Where are you from?

Listen and tick

Listen to the conversation on your audio CD and decide if these sentences are true or false.

		True	False
1	The woman's name is Sophie.	❑	❑
2	She comes from Canada.	❑	❑
3	The man's name is Yiorgos.	❑	❑
4	He comes from Greece.	❑	❑
5	They are already friends.	❑	❑

What does it mean?

Now read the Greek you heard in the conversation and match it with English, as in the example.

I'm from Canada.	Το όνομά μου είναι Λούσυ.
He's from Greece.	Εγώ είμαι από τον Καναδά.
My name's Lucy.	Γειά σας.
What's your name?	Πώς είναι το όνομά σας;
Good evening.	Αυτός είναι από την Ελλάδα.
Hello.	Καλησπέρα.

TOPIC 2: Where are you from?

What does it mean?

Try to work out each of these sentences. It will help if you break them up into the separate words and phrases. Look back at the Key Word panels if you need help.

Then read the sentences out loud when you have figured them out and write the English next to each, as in the example.

1 Το όνομά μου είναι Λούσυ.   <u>My name is Lucy.</u>

2 Είμαι από τον Καναδά.   _____

3 Ο Κώστας είναι από την Ελλάδα.   _____

4 Πώς είναι το όνομά σας;   _____

5 Το όνομά μου είναι Μαρία.   _____

6 Από πού είναι αυτός;   _____

7 Αυτός είναι από την Αγγλία.   _____

8 Αυτή είναι από την Αμερική.   _____

You can compare your pronunciation of the sentences with the models on your audio CD.

TRACK NUMBER
12

Now complete this description of yourself, adding your own details. Then say the description out loud.

Το όνομά μου είναι ... *(name)*.

Εγώ είμαι από τον/την/το ... *(city/town)* στον/στην/στο ... *(country)*.

TOPIC 2: Where are you from?

The Flag Game

① Tear out Game Card 2.

② Find a die and counter(s).

③ Put the counter(s) on START.

④ Throw the die and move that number of squares.

⑤ When you land on a flag, you must ask and answer the appropriate question for that country. For example:

Από πού είστε; **apó poo íste?**
Where are you from?

Είμαι από την Αγγλία.
íme apó tin anglía
I am from England.

⑥ If you can't remember the question or answer, you must go back to the square you came from. You must throw the exact number to finish.

⑦ You can challenge yourself or play with a friend.

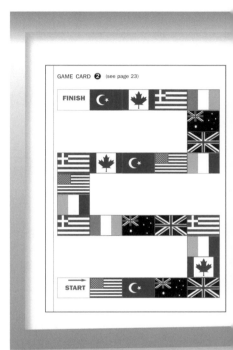

Key Words

η καρέκλα **i karékla** *chair*

το τραπέζι **to trapézi** *table*

η τηλεόραση *television*
i tileórasi

το βιβλίο **to vivlío** *book*

η τσάντα **i tsánta** *bag*

το κομπιούτερ *computer*
to kompiúter

η πόρτα **i pórta** *door*

το παράθυρο *window*
to paráthiro

το στιλό **to stiló** *pen*

το περιοδικό *magazine*
to perioтнikó

ο καναπές **o kanapés** *sofa*

το τηλέφωνο *telephone*
to tiléfono

Listen first to the key words on your CD. Then look around the room you're in and try to use the words to name as many objects as you can find. Count how many Greek words you use.

Then look back at the list and review the words you couldn't remember. Try again to name objects and see if you can beat your first score.

TOPIC 3: What's this?

What does it mean?

Match the Greek with the pictures, then write the pronunciation and the English.

το περιοδικό _____

το βιβλίο _____

η πόρτα _____

το παράθυρο *to paráthiro* window

το στιλό _____

η καρέκλα _____

το τραπέζι _____

η τηλεόραση _____

το τηλέφωνο _____

η τσάντα _____

ο καναπές _____

το κομπιούτερ _____

Word Square

Can you find the seven key words in the word square? Circle them and write the English, as in the example. The words can be horizontal or vertical.

τ	ρ	α	π	έ	ζ	ι	β
η	ί	τ	ό	κ	έ	λ	ι
λ	ο	σ	ρ	α	η	ν	β
έ	ρ	ά	τ	ν	τ	ι	λ
φ	έ	ν	α	α	ο	β	ί
ω	κ	τ	ρ	π	κ	λ	ο
ν	κ	α	ρ	έ	κ	λ	α
ο	ω	ν	έ	ς	σ	ο	η

sofa _____

_____

_____

_____

_____

_____

Odd One Out

Which is the odd one out? Circle the word in each row that doesn't belong.

κομπιούτερ * παράθυρο * καλημέρα * τηλεόραση

η πόρτα * η Ελλάδα * η Αμερική * η Αγγλία

βιβλίο * όνομα * περιοδικό * στιλό

πόλη * καναπές * καρέκλα * τραπέζι

καλησπέρα * γειά σας * καλημέρα * καρέκλα

TOPIC 3: What's this?

Language Focus

○ ○ ○ ○ We have seen that Greek words have three genders: *masculine*, *feminine* and *neuter*. You can't automatically tell what gender a word is, although you will start to spot similarities.

○ ○ ○ ○ The words for "the" and "a" in Greek change according to the gender of the words they refer to (and whether they are singular or plural). The three singular words for "the" are ο **o** *(masculine)*, η **i** *(feminine)*, and το **to** *(neuter)*. The singular words for "a" are ένας **énas** *(masculine)*, μία **mía** *(feminine)*, and ένα **éna** *(neuter)*:

masculine	*feminine*	*neuter*
ο/ένας καναπές	η/μία πόρτα	το/ένα βιβλίο
o/énas kanapés *(sofa)*	**i/mía pórta** *(door)*	**to/éna vivlío** *(book)*
ο/ένας φούρνος	η/μία τηλεόραση	το/ένα όνομα
o/énas foúrnos *(stove)*	**i/mía tileórasi** *(TV)*	**to/éna ónoma** *(name)*
ο/ένας καφές	η/μία τσάντα	το/ένα στιλό
o/énas kafés *(coffee)*	**i/mía tsánta** *(bag)*	**to/éna stiló** *(pen)*

○ ○ ○ To ask what something is, use the phrase: Τι είναι αυτό; **ti íne aftó?** *What is it?* The reply would begin Είναι... **íne...** *(It's...)* followed by what it is with the appropriate form of "a". Note that you don't need to repeat the word for "it" in your answer.

> Τι είναι αυτό; **ti íne aftó?** *What is it?*
>
> Είναι ένα στιλό. **íne éna stiló** *It's a pen.*

○ ○ You can also ask a yes/no question using Αυτό είναι...; **aftó íne...** *(Is it...?)*. The word for "yes" is ναι **ne**, and "no" is όχι **óhi**.

> Αυτό είναι ένα περιοδικό; **aftó íne éna perioτнikó?**
> *Is it a magazine?*
>
> Ναι. Είναι ένα περιοδικό./Όχι. Είναι ένα βιβλίο.
> **ne. íne éna perioτнikó/ohi. íne éna vivlío**
> *Yes. It's a magazine./No, it's a book.*

TOPIC 3: What's this?

Your turn to speak

TRACK NUMBER 14

Now ask what things are.
Follow the prompts on your audio CD.

What is it?

Look at the pictures of everyday objects from unusual angles. Then read the sentences and decide which picture they describe, as in the example.

1 Είναι μία καρέκλα. _e_

2 Είναι ένα κομπιούτερ. __

3 Είναι ένας καναπές. __

4 Είναι ένα τηλέφωνο. __

5 Είναι μία πόρτα. __

6 Είναι μία τηλεόραση. __

7 Είναι ένα στιλό. __

8 Είναι μία τσάντα. __

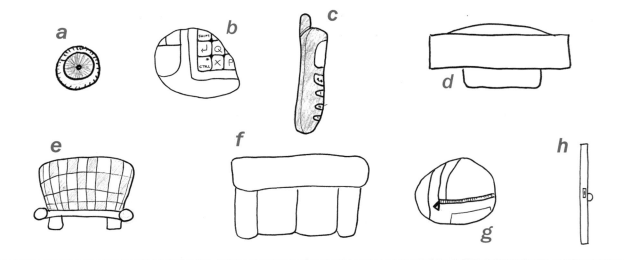

Key Words

το τσάϊ **to tsai**	*tea*	
ο καφές **o kafés**	*coffee*	
το κέϊκ **to keik**	*cake*	
το γλυκό **to glikó**	*sweet*	

το παγωτό **to pagotó**	*ice cream*
το σάντουϊτς **to sándouits**	*sandwich*
η τυρόπιττα **i tirópitta**	*cheese pie*

Language Focus

⊙ ⊙ ⊙ ⊙ The easiest way to ask for something in a café or shop is to use the word θέλω **thélo** *(I want/I would like)*. If you want something else, just add και **ke** *(and)*. It is not impolite in Greek simply to say "I want", rather than "May/Can I have?"

> Θέλω ένα τσάϊ, παρακαλώ. **thélo éna tsai, parakaló**
> *I want/I'd like a tea, please.*
>
> Θέλω ένα κέϊκ και μια τυρόπιττα, παρακαλώ.
> **thélo éna keik ke mia tirópitta, parakaló**
> *I want/I'd like a cake and a cheese pie, please.*

⊙ ⊙ ⊙ ⊙ Masculine words such as καφές **kafés** lose the final **-s** after θέλω **thélo**. The word for "a" also changes from ένας **énas** to έναν **énan**:

> Θέλω έναν καφέ. **thélo énan kafé** *I want/I'd like a coffee.*

⊙ ⊙ ⊙ Having asked for an item you may hear the word ορίστε **oríste** *(here you are)*:

> Θέλω ένα σάντουϊτς, παρακαλώ. **thélo éna**
> **sandouits, parakaló** *I want a sandwich, please.*
>
> Ορίστε, κυρία. **oríste, kiría** *Here you are, Madam.*

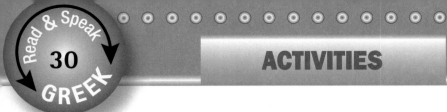
Who orders what?

What are the customers ordering? Listen to your CD and tick what they order, as in the example.

	tea	coffee	sandwich	cake	cheese pie	ice cream	sweet
Customer 1		✔	✔				
Customer 2							
Customer 3							
Customer 4							
Customer 5							

Now look at the table above and pretend you are ordering for yourself, for example:

Θέλω έναν καφέ και ένα σάντουϊτς, παρακαλ.
thélo énan kafé ke éna sándouits, parakaló

TOPIC 3: What's this?

Unscramble the conversation

Can you put this conversation in the correct order?

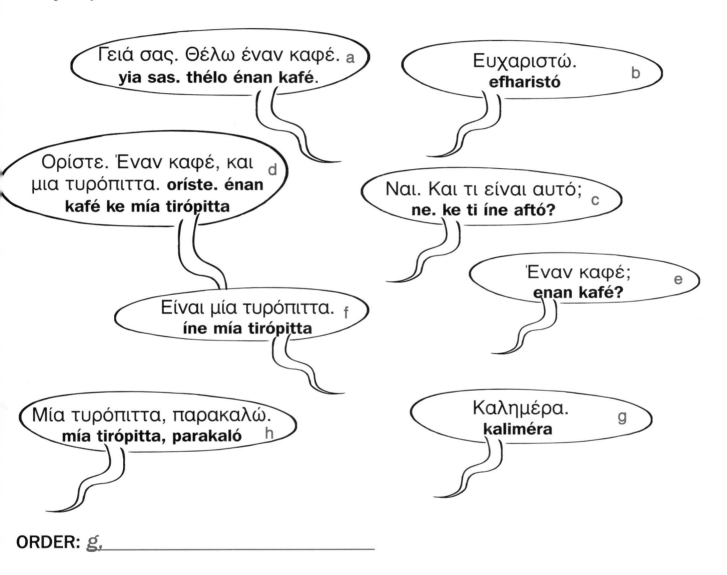

Γειά σας. Θέλω έναν καφέ. a
yia sas. thélo énan kafé.

Ευχαριστώ.
efharistó b

Ορίστε. Έναν καφέ, και
μια τυρόπιτα. **oríste. énan
kafé ke mía tirópitta** d

Ναι. Και τι είναι αυτό;
ne. ke ti íne aftó? c

Είναι μία τυρόπιτα. f
íne mía tirópitta

Έναν καφέ; e
enan kafé?

Μία τυρόπιτα, παρακαλώ.
mía tirópitta, parakaló h

Καλημέρα. g
kaliméra

ORDER: g,_____

Now check your answer with the conversation on your audio CD.

TRACK NUMBER
17

TOPIC 3: What's this?

At the café

TRACK NUMBER

18

Your turn to order now. Look at the menu (κατάλογος) below and then you'll be ready to order from the waiter on your CD.

*** κατάλογος ***

τσάϊ

καφές

σάντουϊτς

κεϊκ

γλυκό

τυρόπιττα

παγωτό

TOPIC 3: What's this?

The Café Game

1. Cut out the picture cards from Game Card 3.

2. Put the cards into a bag.

3. Shake the bag.

4. Pull out a card without looking.

5. Ask for the item on the card. For example:
   Θέλω ένα τσάϊ, παρακαλώ.
   thélo éna tsai, parakaló
   (I want a tea, please.)

6. If you can ask the question out loud quickly and fluently, then put the card aside. If not, then put it back into the bag.

7. See how long it takes you to get all of the cards out of the bag. Or play with a friend and see who can collect the most cards.

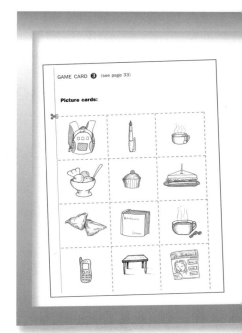

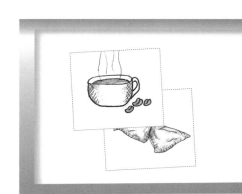

Key Words

TRACK NUMBER
19

το δωμάτιο **to** тнo**mátio** *room*

το ψυγείο **to psiyío** *refrigerator*

η κουρτίνα **i kourtína** *curtain*

ο φούρνος **o foúrnos** *stove*

το κρεβάτι **to kreváti** *bed*

το κάδρο **to kádro** *picture*

το σπίτι **to spíti** *house*

το ντουλάπι
to doulápi *cupboard*

το δέντρο **to** тн**éndro** *tree*

το αυτοκίνητο
to aftokínito *car*

η γάτα **i gáta** *cat*

ο σκύλος **o skílos** *dog*

το ποντίκι **to pondíki** *mouse*

Language Focus

◉ ◉ ◉ ◉ You'll see in the list above that most of the words are neuter, but four are not. Can you pick out the masculine and feminine words? What helped you do this?

◉ ◉ ◉ You can make some helpful hints for yourself for identifying gender. For example *most* words that end in -ο are neuter, *most* that end in -ος are masculine and *most* that end in -α are feminine. However, don't turn these hints into hard-and-fast rules. There are plenty of exceptions.

TOPIC 4: Where is it?

What does it mean?

Join the Greek to the pronunciation and write down the meaning in English.

ο φούρνος	to kreváti	_____
το κρεβάτι	to kádro	_____
το κάδρο	to spíti	_____
ο σκύλος	to тнοmátio	_____
το ποντίκι	o foúrnos	*stove*
το σπίτι	to psiyío	_____
το ντουλάπι	i gáta	_____
το δέντρο	to pondíki	_____
το αυτοκίνητο	to doulápi	_____
το δωμάτιο	i kourtína	_____
το ψυγείο	to тнéndro	_____
η κουρτίνα	to aftokínito	_____
η γάτα	o skílos	_____

What can you see?

Look at the picture and tick (✔) the things you can see, as in the example.

γάτα ✔	ψυγείο ☐
σκύλος ☐	παράθυρο ☐
φούρνος ☐	κρεβάτι ☐
τραπέζι ☐	κουρτίνα ☐
στιλό ☐	ποντίκι ☐
βιβλίο ☐	πόρτα ☐
περιοδικό ☐	κάδρο ☐
κομπιούτερ ☐	ντουλάπι ☐
τσάντα ☐	καρέκλα ☐

Key Words

TRACK NUMBER
20

σε **se**	*in/on*	μπροστά από *in front of* **brostá apó**		
μέσα σε **mesa se**	*inside*			
κάτω από **káto apó**	*under*	πίσω από **píso apó**	*behind*	
πάνω από **páno apó**	*above*	δίπλα σε **THípla se**	*next to*	

Language Focus

⊙ ⊙ ⊙ ⊙ ⊙ In Greek, prepositions ("position" words) are followed by a different form of the word for "the" or "a". The "normal" (subject) forms of "the" and "a" are shown on page 27. After a preposition, the masculine ο **o** becomes τον **ton**, the feminine η **i** becomes την **tin**, but the neuter το **to** stays the same. Sometimes the ending of the following word will also change slightly, e.g. ο καναπές **o kanapés** *(the sofa)* but κάτω από τον καναπέ **káto apó ton kanapé** *(under the sofa)*.

⊙ ⊙ ⊙ ⊙ When you use the preposition σε **se** *(in/on)* with the word for "the", it combines to produce στον/στην/στο **ston/stin/sto**.

η γάτα είναι κάτω από τον καναπέ. **i gáta íne káto apó ton kanapé** *The cat is under the sofa.*

Το στιλό είναι στο τραπέζι. **to stiló íne sto trapézi** *The pen is on the table.*

Practice saying where things are on your CD.

TRACK NUMBER
21

Which word?

Put a circle around the alternative that correctly describes each picture, as in the example.

1 Το αυτοκίνητο είναι (μπροστά από) το σπίτι.
πίσω από

2 Η τηλεόραση είναι πάνω από το παράθυρο.
κάτω από

3 Το κάδρο είναι μπροστά από τον καναπέ.
πάνω από

4 Το κομπιούτερ είναι σ(ε) το τραπέζι.
δίπλα σ(ε)

5 Ο σκύλος είναι πίσω από την καρέκλα.
κάτω από

6 Το ψυγείο είναι δίπλα σ(ε) τον φούρνο.
πάνω από

7 Ο σκύλος είναι μέσα σ(ε) το αυτοκίνητο.
επάνω σ(ε)

Language Focus

A useful phrase in Greek to say what there is in a place is Υπάρχει **ipárhi** *there is:*

> Υπάρχει ένα κομπιούτερ στο τραπέζι.
> **ipárhi éna kompiúter sto trapézi**
> *There's a computer on the table.*
>
> Υπάρχει μια τηλεόραση δίπλα στον καναπέ.
> **ipárhi mía tileórasi τΗípla ston kanapé**
> *There's a television next to the sofa.*
>
> Υπάρχει ένα κάδρο κάτω από το παράθυρο.
> **ipárhi éna kádro káto apó to paráthiro**
> *There's a picture under the window.*

If you want to ask the question *Is there a ...?*, you can use the same phrase, raising your voice at the end.

> Υπάρχει μια τηλεόραση στο δωμάτιο;
> **ipárhi mía tileórasi sto τΗomátio?**
> *Is there a television in the room?*

Look around the room you are in at the moment, or think of a room you know well. Can you describe where some of the things are, using Υπάρχει... **ipárhi...?**

TOPIC 4: Where is it?

Where are the mice?

See how many mice you can find in the picture and make sentences about them using the sentence table, as in this example:

Υπάρχει ένα ποντίκι μπροστά στον φούρνο. **ipárhi éna pondiki brostá ston foúrno**

There's a mouse in front of the stove.

		το τραπέζι.
		την καρέκλα.
		το ψυγείο.
	μέσα σ(ε)	τον καναπέ.
	πάνω από	το ντουλάπι.
Υπάρχει ένα ποντίκι	κάτω από	τον φούρνο.
	πίσω από	την τηλεόραση.
	σ(ε)	το κομπιούτερ.
	δίπλα σ(ε)	το κρεβάτι.
	μπροστά από	

Language Focus

Plurals of Greek words vary according to gender, so you will need to learn their endings individually. The word for "the" also changes to οι **i** for masculine and feminine plurals and τα **ta** for neuter plurals. Here are some words you know already with their plurals. You may be able to spot some similarities in the plural patterns.

	singular	*plural*
table	το τραπέζι **trapézi**	τα τραπέζια **trapézya**
chair	η καρέκλα **karékla**	οι καρέκλες **karékles**
refrigerator	το ψυγείο **psiyío**	τα ψυγεία **psiyía**
sofa	ο καναπές **kanapés**	οι καναπέδες **kanapéthes**
cupboard	το ντουλάπι **doolápi**	τα ντουλάπια **doolápya**
stove	ο φούρνος **foúrnos**	οι φούρνοι **foúrni**
television	η τηλεόραση **tileórasi**	οι τηλεοράσεις **tileórasis**
bed	το κρεβάτι **kreváti**	τα κρεβάτια **krevátya**
book	το βιβλίο **vivlío**	τα βιβλία **vivlía**
bag	η τσάντα **tsánda**	οι τσάντες **tsándes**
door	η πόρτα **pórta**	οι πόρτες **pórtes**
window	το παράθυρο **paráthiro**	τα παράθυρα **paráthira**
pen	το στιλό **stiló**	τα στιλό* **stiló** (*no change)
room	το δωμάτιο **thomátio**	τα δωμάτια **thomátyo**
curtain	η κουρτίνα **koortína**	οι κουρτίνες **koortínes**
picture	το κάδρο **káthro**	τα κάδρα **káthra**
house	το σπίτι **spíti**	τα σπίτια **spítya**
tree	το δέντρο **théndro**	τα δέντρα **théndra**
dog	ο σκύλος **skílo**	οι σκύλοι **skíli**
cat	η γάτα **gáta**	οι γάτες **gátes**
mouse	το ποντίκι **pondíki**	τα ποντίκια **pondíkya**

Note that υπάρχει **ipárhi** (*there is*) changes to υπάρχουν **ipárhoon** (*there are*) if you are talking about more than one thing: Υπάρχουν βιβλία στο ντουλάπι. **ipárhoon vivlía sto doolápi** (*There are books in the cupboard.*)

TOPIC 4: Where is it?

○ ○ ○ You can make a sentence negative in Greek by inserting the word δεν **THen** (meaning *not*) in front of the verb. For example:

> Είμαι απο την Αγγλία. Δεν είμαι από την Αμερική.
> **íme apó tin anglía. THen íme apó tin amerikí**
> *I am from England. I am not from America.*
>
> Δεν υπάρχει ένα κομπιούτερ στο δωμάτιο.
> **THen ipárhi éna kompiúter sto THomátio**
> *There isn't a computer in the room.*

Listen and learn

TRACK NUMBER
22

You'll find an activity on your CD to help you remember the plurals.

True or False?

Decide if the sentences describing the picture are true or false, as in the example.

		True	False
1	Υπάρχει ένα ψυγείο στο δωμάτιο.	☑	☐
2	Υπάρχει ένα κρεβάτι στο δωμάτιο.	☐	☐
3	Το τηλέφωνο είναι στο τραπέζι.	☐	☐
4	Δεν υπάρχουν ντουλάπια.	☐	☐
5	Υπάρχουν παράθυρα.	☐	☐
6	Δεν υπάρχει ένα ποντίκι κάτω από το τραπέζι.	☐	☐
7	Υπάρχουν δέντρα πίσω από το σπίτι.	☐	☐
8	Ο φούρνος είναι δίπλα στο ψυγείο.	☐	☐
9	Υπάρχει ένας σκύλος κάτω από το τραπέζι.	☐	☐
10	Δεν υπάρχει μια τηλεόραση στο δωμάτιο.	☐	☐

TOPIC 4: Where is it?

Language Review

You're half way through *Read and Speak Greek for Beginners* – congratulations! This is a good time to summarize the main language points covered so far.

1 Greek has three genders: *masculine, feminine* and *neuter*. You can often tell the gender of a word by its ending. Some masculine nouns end in —ος **-os**; some feminine nouns in —α **-a** or —η **-i**; some neuter nouns in —ο **-o**.

2 The words for "a" and "the" (*articles*) change according to the gender. When the person or object is the subject of the sentence, the forms of the articles are:

article	masculine	feminine	neuter
a/an	ένας **énas**	μία **mía**	ένα **éna**
the	ο **o**	η **i**	το **to**

Υπάρχει ένας φούρνος δίπλα στο ψυγείο.
iparhi énas foúrnos тнípla sto psiyío
There's a stove next to the refrigerator.

Υπάρχει μία τσάντα και ένα στιλό στο ντουλάπι.
iparhi mia tsanda ke éna stiló sto doolápi
There's a bag and a pen in the cupboard.

3 When the noun is *not* the subject of the sentence, the articles can change:

article	masculine	feminine	neuter
a/an	έναν **énan**	μία **mía**	ένα **éna**
the	τον **ton**	την **tin**	το **to**

Θέλω έναν καφέ, παρακαλώ.
thélo énan kafé, parakaló   *I'd like a coffee. please.*

Είμαι από την Αθήνα.
íme apó tin athína   *I'm from (the) Athens.*

4 Plurals vary but there are some patterns: masculine nouns ending in —ος form the plural with —οι **-i**; feminine nouns ending in -α or —η form the plural with —ες **-es**; neuter nouns ending in —ο form the plural with —α **-a** (see page 40).

TOPIC 4: Where is it?

My room

1. Tear out Game Card 4 at the back of your book and cut out the the small pictures of items around the house (leave the sentence-build cards at the bottom of the sheet for the moment).

2. Stick the pictures wherever you like on the scene below.

3. Cut out the sentence-build cards from Game Card 4. Make and say aloud as many sentences as you can describing your room. For example:

| Υπάρχει | ένα κάδρο | πάνω από το | κρεβάτι | . |

iparhi éna káтнro páno apó to kreváti
There's a picture above the bed.

Key Words

μεγάλος **megálos**	*big*	
μικρός **micrós**	*small*	
παλιός **paliós**	*old*	
καινούριος **kenoórios**	*new*	
πολύ **polí**	*very*	

ακριβός **akrivós**	*expensive*	
φτηνός **ftinós**	*inexpensive*	
αργός **argós**	*slow*	
γρήγορος **grígoros**	*fast*	

Can you remember?

Cover the Key Words panel above. Then see if you can write out the pronunciation and meaning of the words below, as in the example.

αργός **a** *r* g **ó** <u>s</u>   <u>slow</u>

μικρός **m** _ _ _ _ **s**   ———

φτηνός **f** _ _ _ **ó** _   ———

ακριβός _ **k** _ _ _ **ó** _   ———

καινούριος _ **e** _ _ **ú** _ _ _ _   ———

παλιός **p** _ _ _ _ _ _   ———

πολύ _ _ _ **í**   ———

γρήγορος **g** _ **í** _ _ **r** _ _   ———

μεγάλος **m** _ _ _ **l** _ _   ———

Language Focus

◉ ◉ ◉ ◉ In Greek, descriptive words (adjectives) come before the word they are describing, as they do in English:

> ένας μεγάλος σκύλος **énas megalos skílos** *a big dog*
>
> ο παλιός καναπές **énas paliós kanapés** *the old sofa*

◉ ◉ ◉ ◉ Adjectives change their ending depending on the gender of the word they describe. The adjectives shown in the panel on page 44 are masculine. In general, adjectives that end in -ος (**-os**) for masculine words will change to -η (**-i**) or -α (**-a**) when describing feminine words and to -ο (**-o**) for neuter words.

> η μεγάλη καρέκλα **i megáli karékla** *the big chair (fem.)*
>
> ένα μεγάλο σπίτι **éna megálo spíti** *a big house (neuter)*
>
> μία παλιά τσάντα **mía paliá tsánda** *an old bag (fem.)*
>
> το παλιό τραπέζι **to palió trapézi** *the old table (neuter)*

◉ ◉ ◉ You can add πολύ **polí** *(very)* before the adjective, just like in English:

> Το σπίτι είναι πολύ μικρό. **to spíti íne polí mikró** *The house is very small.*
>
> Η τσάντα δεν είναι πολύ ακριβή. **i tsánda тнen íne polí akriví** *The bag isn't very expensive.*
>
> Ο καφές είναι πολύ φτηνός. **O kafés íne polí ftinós** *The coffee is very inexpensive.*

◉ ◉ Adjectives endings also change for the plural. You don't need to worry now about the rules, but it's useful to know what is happening. Here are some examples:

> τα μικρά σπίτια **ta mikrá spítya** *the small houses*
>
> οι ακριβές τσάντες **i akrivés tsándes** *the expensive bags*

What does it mean?

Match the Greek with the pictures. Then read the Greek out loud and write the English next to each, as in the example.

ένα μεγάλο σάντουϊτς _____

ένα μικρό ποντίκι _____

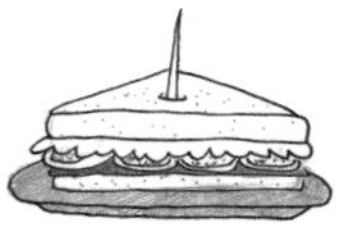

ένας μικρός σκύλος _____(a) small dog_____

ένας καινούριος καναπές _____

ένα μεγάλο δέντρο _____

ένα πολύ παλιό αυτοκίνητο _____

ένα φτηνό κάδρο _____

ένας μικρός καφές _____

TOPIC 5: What's it like?

Listen and tick

Listen to the conversation at the car rental company and decide if these sentences are true or false.

TRACK NUMBER
24

	True	False
1 The conversation takes place in the evening.	☐	☐
2 The woman wants to rent a car.	☐	☐
3 She thinks the first car is too expensive.	☐	☐
4 She thinks the second car is too big.	☐	☐
5 She likes the third car.	☐	☐

Unscramble the sentences

Look at the scrambled sentences below and identify the correct order, as in the example.

1 ένα / αυτοκίνητο / θέλω   3 / 1 / 2

2 είναι / το αυτοκίνητο / δεν / μεγάλο / πολύ   ☐ / ☐ / ☐ / ☐ / ☐

3 το αυτοκίνητο / ακριβό / είναι   ☐ / ☐ / ☐

4 το όνομά / Μαρία / μου / Βαζάκα / είναι   ☐ / ☐ / ☐ / ☐ / ☐

5 εγώ / την Αθήνα / από / είμαι   ☐ / ☐ / ☐ / ☐

Language Focus

To talk about what you and other people have, the most useful phrases are έχω **ého** *(I have)*, έχει **éhi** *(he/she/it has)*, and έχουμε **éhoome** *(we have)*:

> Έχω έναν μεγάλο σκύλο.
> **ého énan megalo skílo**
>
> *I have a big dog.*
>
> Αυτός έχει ένα παλιό σπίτι στο Λονδίνο.
> **Aftós éhi ena palió spíti sto LonтHíno**
>
> *He has an old house in London.*
>
> Έχουμε ένα καινούριο αυτοκίνητο.
> **éhoume ena kenoúrio aftokínito**
>
> *We have a new car.*

You could also ask Έχετε...; **éhete...?** *(Do you have...?)*:

> Έχετε ένα φτηνό αυτοκίνητο;
> **éhete éna ftinó aftokínito?**
>
> *Do you have an inexpensive car?*
>
> Έχετε ένα στιλό;
> **éhete éna stiló?**
>
> *Do you have a pen?*

TRACK NUMBER
25

Now you can take part in a conversation with the car rental company. Follow the prompts on your audio CD.

Key Words

το πόδι **to pótHi**	*leg*	το κεφάλι **to kefáli**	*head*
το χέρι **to héri**	*arm*	η μύτη **i míti**	*nose*
τα μάτια **ta mátia**	*eyes*	το στόμα **to stóma**	*mouth*
τα αυτιά **ta aftiá**	*ears*	το στομάχι **to stomáhi**	*stomach*
τα μαλλιά **ta maliá**	*hair*	η ουρά **i oorá**	*tail*

NOTE: τα **ta** means "the" when referring to (neuter) plural words.

By now you're probably feeling much more confident about reading and speaking Greek. Maybe you'd like to try writing the Greek letters for yourself. Although it's fun to copy and key the letters, you will need a guide to writing Greek in order to make sure you are forming them correctly. Handwritten Greek can also look significantly different from printed. (See page 89 for the Greek script and alphabet.)

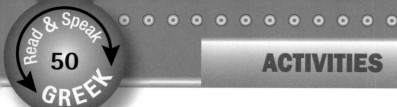

Which word?

Circle the correct word to match the translation,
as in the example.

1	*head*	πολύ	(κεφάλι)	καρέκλα	κρεβάτι
2	*leg*	δέντρο	αυτός	αργός	πόδι
3	*stomach*	σκύλος	γάτα	καφές	στομάχι
4	*mouth*	στόμα	πού	στιλό	ντουλάπι
5	*tail*	βιβλίο	σπίτι	ουρά	δωμάτιο
6	*hair*	ποντίκι	μικρός	κάδρα	μαλλιά
7	*ears*	αυτή	αυτιά	είναι	τσάντα
8	*nose*	μύτη	από	εγώ	γρήγορος
9	*eyes*	είμαι	μάτια	ψυγείο	παλιός
10	*arm*	παλιός	έχει	χέρι	τραπέζι

TOPIC 5: What's it like?

At the circus

Can you use the words in the box to complete the description
of the clowns, Carlos and Carlotta?

1 μεγάλο

2 μεγάλη

3 μικρή

4 παλιά

5 μικρό

6 μικρά

Ο Κάρλος έχει _____ μάτια και ένα _____ στομάχι.

Έχει μια _____ τσάντα στο χέρι.

Η Καρλόττα έχει μια _____ μύτη και ένα _____ στόμα.

Έχει μια _____ γάτα.

What does it look like?

What does the alien look like? Make as many sentences as you can describing what this creature looks like.

We've included some more adjectives you could use to describe his features.

Example

Αυτός έχει ένα χοντρό στομάχι.
aftós éhi éna hondró stomáhi
He has a fat stomach.

beautiful	όμορφος/-η/-ο
	ómorfos/-i/-o
ugly	άσκημος/-η/-ο
	áskimos/-i/-o
fat	χοντρός/-ή/-ό
	hondrós/-í/-ó
thin	λεπτός/-ή/-ό
	leptós/-í/-ó
long	μακρύς/-ιά/-ύ
	makrís/-yá/-í
short	κοντός/-ή/-ό
	kondós/-í/-ó
strange	παράξενος/-η/-ο
	paráksenos/-i/-o

What do you have?

1. Cut out set 1 picture cards from Game Card 5 and put them in a bag.

2. Cut out set 2 adjective cards and put them in a different bag.

3. Pull out one card from each bag without looking.

4. Make a sentence to match the cards you have chosen, for example:

   Εχω ένα παλιό κομπιούτερ.
   ého éna palió kompiúter
   (*I have an old computer.*)

   Don't forget to change the ending of the adjective for a feminine or neuter item.

5. If the adjective can't be used with that picture, put both cards back and try again. Keep playing until all the cards have been chosen.

6. You can put the cards back in the bag and start again – each time the sentences will be different.

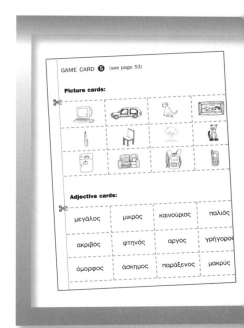

Key Words

TRACK NUMBER
27

το αεροδρόμιο **to aerotнrómio** (pl. αεροδρόμια)	airport	η γέφυρα **i yéfira** (pl. γέφυρες)	bridge
το σχολείο **to skolío** (pl. σχολεία)	school	ο δρόμος **o тнrómos** (pl. δρόμοι)	street
το ξενοδοχείο **to ksenoтнohío** (pl. ξενοδοχεία)	hotel	το μουσείο **to moosío** (pl. μουσεία)	museum
η τράπεζα **i trápeza** (pl. τράπεζες)	bank	το νοσοκομείο **to nosokomío** (pl. νοσοκομεία)	hospital
το εστιατόριο **to estiatório** (pl. εστιατόρια)	restaurant	η στάση **i stási** (pl. στάσεις)	bus stop
ο σταθμός **o stathmós** (pl. σταθμοί)	station	πού; **poo?**	where?
		κοντά σε **kontá se**	near
το πάρκο **to párko** (pl. πάρκα)	park	απέναντι από **apénandi apó**	opposite

TRACK NUMBER
28

You are new in town and are asking a Greek friend about the facilities. Follow the prompts on your audio CD.

TOPIC 6: How do I get there?

Language Focus

◎ ◎ ◎ ◎ Modern Greek has many loan words from other languages, particularly English, but also French. Some examples of these are κομπιούτερ **kompiúter** *(computer)*, ασανσέρ **asansér** *(elevator,* from the French *"ascenseur")*, σάντουϊτς **sandouits** *(sandwich)*.

◎ ◎ ◎ ◎ In many cases, the English word itself derives from ancient Greek and then comes back into the language later! Some examples of this are: τηλέφωνο **tiléfono** *telephone* (literally "far voice"); γεωγραφία **yeografía** *geography* (literally "world drawing"). Think of "politics" – that comes from πολιτική **politikí** – something that relates to the word "city" (πόλη **póli**).

Questions and answers

Match the questions with their answers, as in the example.

Πού είναι η τράπεζα;

Υπάρχει ένα εστιατόριο;

Υπάρχει ένα ξενοδοχείο;

Πού είναι το νοσοκομείο;

Πού είναι η γέφυρα;

Το νοσοκομείο είναι κοντά στο σχολείο.

Υπάρχει ένα ξενοδοχείο μπροστά από το σταθμό.

Ναι, υπάρχει ένα εστιατόριο.

Η γέφυρα είναι εκεί.

Η τράπεζα είναι δίπλα στο σχολείο.

Key Words

TRACK NUMBER
29

το ταξί **to taksí**   *taxi*
(pl. ταξί)

το αεροπλάνο   *plane*
to aeropláno (pl. αεροπλάνα)

το λεωφορείο   *bus*
to leoforío (pl. λεωφορεία)

το ποδήλατο   *bicycle*
to poᴛʜílato (pl. ποδήλατα)

το τρένο **to tréno**   *train*
(pl. τρένα)

το πλοίο **to plío**   *boat*
(pl. πλοία)

Language Focus

To express how you travel, use με **me**, meaning "with", but you have to insert the word for "the" before the means of transport:

με το λεωφορείο **me to leoforío**   *by bus*

με το τρένο **me to tréno**   *by train*

με το αεροπλάνο **me to aeropláno**   *by plane*

με το πλοίο **me to plío**   *by boat*

με τα πόδια **me ta pόᴛʜia**   *on foot (literally, "with the feet")*

TOPIC 6: How do I get there?

Word Square

Can you find the seven different means of transportation in the word square? Write out the pronunciation and meaning for the words you have found, as in the example.

α	λ	υ	κ	η	τ.	υ	ν	α
κ	ε	τ	α	μ	σ	η	α	υ
υ	ω	τ	α	ξ	ί	σ	ε	τ
η	φ	ρ	ξ	ρ	ε	δ	ρ	ο
π	ο	δ	ή	λ	α	τ	ο	κ
ό	ρ	ν	ε	ι	τ	α	π	ί
δ	ε	ο	η	κ	ρ	ε	λ	ν
ι	ί	α	σ	λ	έ	τ	ά	η
τ	ο	η	υ	α	ν	ρ	ν	τ
λ	ε	ω	π	λ	ο	ί	ο	ο

taksi *(taxi)*

_____

_____

_____

_____

_____

_____

PLURALS

Language Focus

⊙ ⊙ ⊙ ⊙ ⊙ You have seen that plurals of Greek nouns have different endings from the singular and need to be learnt individually. However, there are some general rules that may help you.

⊙ ⊙ ⊙ ⊙ ⊙ Some masculine words end in —ος **-os**. Plurals of these words end in —οι **-i**.

> Υπάρχουν σκύλοι στο πάρκο.
> **ipárhoon skíli sto párko**
> *There are dogs in the park.*

⊙ ⊙ ⊙ ⊙ ⊙ Some feminine words end in —α **–a**. Plurals of these words end in -ες **–es**.

> Υπάρχουν γάτες στο δωμάτιο.
> **ipárhoon gátes sto τhomátio**
> *There are cats in the room.*

⊙ ⊙ ⊙ ⊙ ⊙ Some neuter words end in -ο **–o**. Plurals of these words end in -α **-a**.

> Υπάρχουν βιβλία στο ντουλάπι.
> **ipárhoon vivlía sto doolápi**
> *There are books in the cupboard.*

⊙ ⊙ ⊙ ⊙ ⊙ The word for "the" also changes for plural words:

	As the subject	As the object
masc.	οι σκύλοι **i skíli**	τους σκύλους **tous skílous** (the dogs)
fem.	οι τσάντες **i tsándes**	τις τσάντες **tis tsándes** (the bags)
neuter	τα μάτια **ta mátia**	τα μάτια **ta mátia** (the eyes)

TOPIC 6: How do I get there?

Key Words

TRACK NUMBER
30

συγνώμη — *excuse me!*
signómi

πώς πάω στον/στην/στο…
pos pao ston/stin/sto…
How do I get to …?

πηγαίνετε… — *go…*
piyénete…

στρίψτε… — *turn…*
stípste…

δεξιά **deksiá** — *right/on the right*

αριστερά — *left/on the left*
aristerái

ευθεία **efthía** — *straight ahead*

πάρτε τον πρώτο δρόμο
párte ton próto тнrómo
take the first street

πάρτε τον δεύτερο δρόμο
párte ton тнéftero тнrómo
take the second street

εδώ **eтнó** — *here*

εκεί **ekí** — *there*

μετά **metá** — *then/after that*

TRACK NUMBER
31

Ask for directions to places around town.
Follow the prompts on your audio CD.

Which way?

Make questions and answers, as in the example.

Συγνώμη. Πώς πάω στο σταθμό;
signómi. pos pao sto stathmó?
Excuse me, how do I get to the station?

Πάρτε τον πρώτο δρόμο αριστερά.
párte ton próto ᴛʜʀómo **aristerá**
Take the first street on the left.

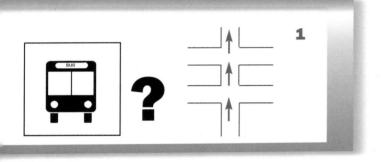

1

2

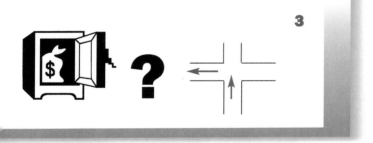

3

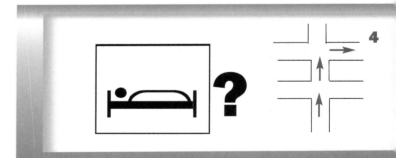

4

5

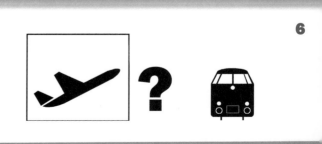

6

TOPIC 6: How do I get there?

Around town

Below is a plan of a small town with some landmarks shown.
Starting from *You are here*, try to give directions to the following places:

ο σταθμός	το ξενοδοχείο Βύρωνας	το πάρκο	η στάση
o stathmós	**to ksenoτΗοhío Víronas**	**to párko**	**i stási**
the station	*the hotel Byron*	*the park*	*the bus stop*

For example, your directions to the station could be something like this:

Πηγαίνετε ευθεία από εδώ. Μετά, πάρτε τον πρώτο δρόμο δεξιά στην τράπεζα. Ο σταθμός είναι κοντά στην γέφυρα.

piyénete efthía apó eΤΗό. metá, párte ton próto ΤΗrómo deksiá stin trápeza. o staτΗmós íne kontá stin yéfira

Go straight ahead from here. After that, take the first street on the right at the bank. The station is near the bridge.

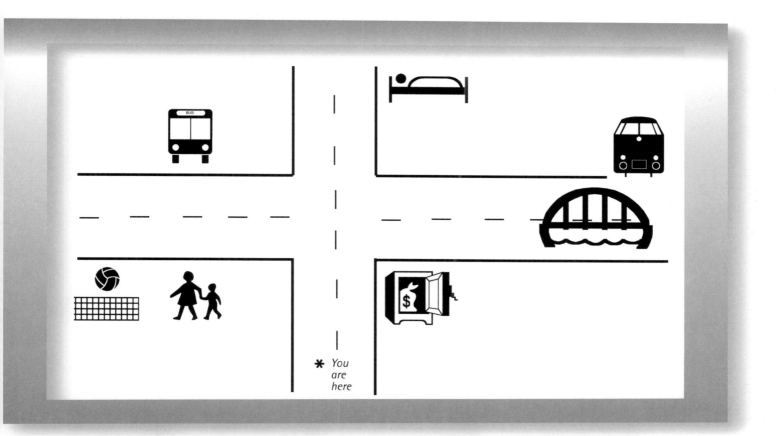

ACTIVITIES

Unscramble the conversation

See if you can read the Greek in the word balloons. Then put the conversation into the correct order.

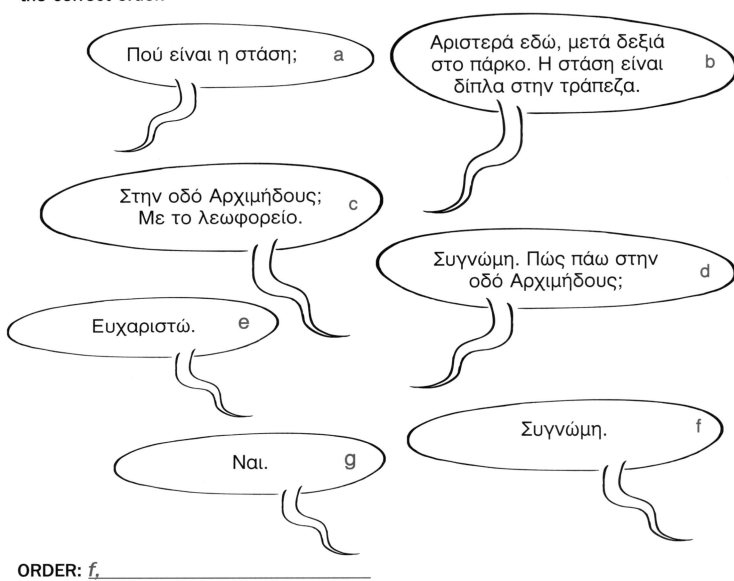

Πού είναι η στάση;   a

Αριστερά εδώ, μετά δεξιά στο πάρκο. Η στάση είναι δίπλα στην τράπεζα.   b

Στην οδό Αρχιμήδους; Με το λεωφορείο.   c

Συγνώμη. Πώς πάω στην οδό Αρχιμήδους;   d

Ευχαριστώ.   e

Συγνώμη.   f

Ναι.   g

ORDER: *f,*_____

Check your answer with the conversation on your audio CD.

TRACK NUMBER
32

TOPIC 6: How do I get there?

Town Planning

TRACK NUMBER
33

1. Cut out the pictures of places around town from Game Card 6.

2. Listen to the first set of directions for the bank on your audio CD.

3. Pause the CD and stick the picture of the bank in the correct place on the town map on your game card.

4. Listen to the next set of directions and stick down the appropriate picture.

5. Repeat for all the directions until you have all your pictures stuck down on the map.

6. Looking at the completed map, you could try to give directions to the various places yourself. For example:

Πάρτε τον δεύτερο δρόμο αριστερά.
Η τράπεζα είναι δεξιά, δίπλα στο σχολείο.

párte ton ᴛʜéftero ᴛʜrómo aristerá
i trápeza íne ᴛʜeksiá, ᴛʜípla sto skolío

(Take the second street on the left.
The bank is on the right, next to the school.)

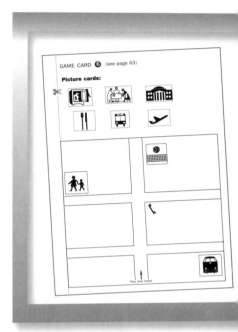

Key Words

η γυναίκα **i yinéka**	*wife*	η κόρη **i kóri** (pl. οι κόρες)	*daughter*
ο άντρας **o ántras**	*husband*	ο γιός **o yiós** (pl. οι γιοί)	*son*
η μητέρα **i mitéra**	*mother*		
ο πατέρας **o patéras**	*father*	η αδελφή **i aτнelfí** (pl. οι αδελφές)	*sister*
το παιδί **to pedí** (pl. τα παιδιά)	*child*	ο αδελφός **o aτнelfós** (pl. οι αδελφοί)	*brother*

Language Focus

⊙ ⊙ ⊙ ⊙ ⊙ You saw the verb έχω **ého** (*I have*) earlier on page 48. You can also use this verb to talk about your family.

> Έχω μία αδελφή και έναν αδελφό.
>
> **ého mía aτнelfí ke énan aτнelfó**
>
> *I have a sister and a brother.*

⊙ ⊙ ⊙ ⊙ **To say what you *don't* have, you just insert the word** δεν **then**, **meaning** *not*, **in front of the verb:**

> Δεν έχω μία αδελφή.
> **тнen ého mía aтнelfí**
> *I don't have a sister .*
>
> Δεν έχουμε παιδιά.
> **тнen éhoome peтнiá**
> *We don't have children.*

What does it mean?

Join the English to the pronunciation and the Greek script, as in the example.

children	**aтнelfés**	κόρες
husband	**mitéra**	αδελφές
brother	**kóres**	γιός
daughter	**pediá**	αδελφοί
mother	**patéras**	γυναίκα
sister	**pedí**	άντρας
brothers	**yí**	μητέρα
wife	**aтнelfí**	παιδιά
sons	**kóri**	πατέρας
child	**yiós**	αδελφός
sisters	**yinéka**	παιδί
son	**ántras**	αδελφή
daughters	**aтнelfí**	κόρη
father	**aтнelfós**	γιοί

TOPIC 7: Who's this?

Language Focus

You already know the words for *I, you, he* and *she*, and how to say *my* and *your*. Here are the other pronouns and "possession" words:

pronoun			possession word		
I	εγώ	**egó**	*my*	μου	**moo**
*you**	εσύ	**esí**	*your*	σου	**soo**
he	αυτός	**aftós**	*his*	του	**too**
she	αυτή	**aftí**	*her*	της	**tis**
it	αυτό	**aftó**	*its*	του	**too**
we	εμείς	**emís**	*our*	μας	**mas**
*you**	εσείς	**esís**	*your*	σας	**sas**
they (m)	αυτοί	**aftí**	*their (m)*	τους	**toos**
they (f)	αυτές	**aftés**	*their (f)*	τους	**toos**
they (n)	αυτά	**aftá**	*their (n)*	τους	**toos**

Possession words come after the noun (with "the"):

ο αδελφός μου **o aᴛʜelfós moo** *my brother ("the brother my")*

η αδελφή της **i aᴛʜelfí tis** *her sister*

ο πατέρας μας **o patéras mas** *our father*

η μητέρα τους **i mitéra toos** *their mother*

TOPIC 7: Who's this?

◎ ◎ ◎ **If you want to introduce someone, you can use the simple phrase** εδώ είναι **eτнó íne** *("here is …").* **You need to add** Ο **o** *(masc.)* **or** η **i** *(fem.)* **before the name.**

> Εδώ είναι ο αδελφός μου, ο Γιάννης.
> **eτнó íne o aτнelfós moo, o Yiánnis**
> *This is my brother, Giannis. ["here is my brother, Giannis"]*
>
> Εδώ είναι η αδελφή μου, η Άννα.
> **eτнó íne i aτнelfí moo, i Anna**
> *This is my sister, Anna. ["here is my sister, Anna"]*

Family Tree

Look at the family tree and imagine you are one of the members of the family.

Make up sentences about your relatives, for example:

Εδώ είναι η κόρη μου, η Ελένη. **eτнó íne i kóri moo, i Eléni**
This is my daughter, Eleni.

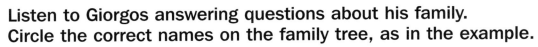

Giorgos's family

Listen to Giorgos answering questions about his family.
Circle the correct names on the family tree, as in the example.

Παύλος
Κώστας
Γιώργος

Αντρέα
Ελένη
Μαρία

(Γιώργος)
Κώστας
Χάρρυ

Γιάννης
Παύλος
Κώστας

Questions and answers

Now read the questions on the left and then match them to the answers on the right that Robert gave, as in the example.

1 Έχεις αδελφούς;

2 Πώς είναι το όνομα
  της μητέρας σου;

3 Έχεις αδελφές;

4 Πώς είναι το όνομα του
  αδελφού σου;

5 Πώς είναι το όνομα του
  πατέρα σου;

6 Πώς είναι το όνομά σου;

7 Από πού είσαι;

a Το όνομά της είναι Μαρία.

b Όχι. Δεν έχω αδελφές.

c Το όνομά του είναι Κώστας.

d Είμαι από την Χαλκίδα.

e Το όνομά μου είναι Γιώργος.

f Το όνομά του είναι Παύλος.

g Ναι. Έχω έναν αδελφό

TOPIC 7: Who's this?

Language Focus

Who? is Ποιός; **piós?**:

> Ποιός είναι αυτός; **piós íne aftós?** *Who's this?*

Remember how to say *"pleased to meet you"* from Topic 1:
χαίρω πολύ **héro polí**

You can put all this together to make a short conversation:

> – Γειά σου, Άννα.
> **yiásoo, Ánna**
> *Hello, Anna.*
>
> – Γειά σου, Αντρέα. Ποιός είναι αυτός;
> **yiásoo, Andréa. piós íne aftós?**
> *Hello, Andrea. Who's this?*
>
> – Εδώ είναι ο αδελφός μου, ο Γιάννης.
> **етнó íne о атнelfós moo, о Yiánnis**
> *This is my brother, Giannis.*
>
> – Γειά σου, Γιάννη. Χαίρω πολύ.
> **yiásou, Yiánni. héro polí**
> *Hello, Gianni. Pleased to meet you..*
>
> – Χαίρω πολύ, Αντρέα.
> **héro polí, Andréa**
> *Pleased to meet you, Andrea.*

TRACK NUMBER
36

Now introduce your family. Follow the prompts on your audio CD.

Key Words

ἕνα	**éna**	one	ἕξι	**éksi**	six
δύο	**THÍo**	two	εφτά	**eftá**	seven
τρία	**tría**	three	οχτώ	**októ**	eight
τέσσερα	**téssera**	four	εννέα	**enéa**	nine
πέντε	**pénde**	five	δέκα	**THÉka**	ten

Language Focus

Numbers in Greek have some special features to do with gender. As you know, the article *a/an* in Greek has three forms. The neuter form ἕνα **éna** is the same as the word for *one* when you are counting in general. However, if the person or thing you are counting is feminine or masculine, the word for *one* changes:

> Έχω μία αδελφή και έναν αδελφό.
> **ého mía aTHelfí ke énan aTHelfó**
> *I have one sister and and one brother.*

The word for *two* does not change in the same way, but *three* and *four* also change according to gender. *Three* is τρεις **tris** for feminine and masculine nouns but τρία **tría** for neuter nouns. *Four* is τέσσερις **téseris** for feminine and masculine nouns, but τέσσερα **tésera** for neuter nouns:

> Έχω τρεις αδελφές και τρία παιδιά.
> **ého tris aTHelfés ke tría peTHiá**
> *I have three sisters and three children.*
>
> Έχουμε τέσσερις αδελφούς και τέσσερα παιδιά.
> **éhoome tésseris aTHelfoós ke téssera peTHiá**
> *We have four brothers and four children.*

TOPIC 7: Who's this?

How many?

Match the numbers to the pronunciation, as in the example.

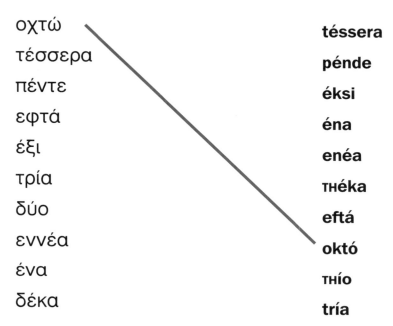

οχτώ	**téssera**
τέσσερα	**pénde**
πέντε	**éksi**
εφτά	**éna**
έξι	**enéa**
τρία	**тнéka**
δύο	**eftá**
εννέα	**októ**
ένα	**тнío**
δέκα	**tría**

Greek sums

Circle the correct answer to these sums, as in the example.

1   ένα + τρία=   ένα δύο τρία (τέσσερα) πέντε έξι εφτά οχτώ εννέα δέκα

2   έξι + δύο =   ένα δύο τρία τέσσερα πέντε έξι εφτά οχτώ εννέα δέκα

3   δύο + ένα =   ένα δύο τρία τέσσερα πέντε έξι εφτά οχτώ εννέα δέκα

4   εφτά + δύο = ένα δύο τρία τέσσερα πέντε έξι εφτά οχτώ εννέα δέκα

5   δύο + πέντε = ένα δύο τρία τέσσερα πέντε έξι εφτά οχτώ εννέα δέκα

6   τρία + τρία = ένα δύο τρία τέσσερα πέντε έξι εφτά οχτώ εννέα δέκα

7   οχτώ + δύο = ένα δύο τρία τέσσερα πέντε έξι εφτά οχτώ εννέα δέκα

8   έξι + τρία =   ένα δύο τρία τέσσερα πέντε έξι εφτά οχτώ εννέα δέκα

9   ένα + εννέα = ένα δύο τρία τέσσερα πέντε έξι εφτά οχτώ εννέα δέκα

My family

Use the table below to make sentences about yourself, as in the examples.

Έχω δύο αδελφές. **ého ᴛʜío aᴛʜelfés**   *I have two sisters.*

Δεν έχω παιδιά. **ᴛʜen ého peᴛʜia**   *I don't have any children.*

	⊙	μία αδελφή
	⊙	δύο αδελφές
	⊙	έναν αδελφό
Έχω	⊙	αδελφούς
	⊙	έναν γιό
	⊙	γιούς
	⊙	μία κόρη
Δεν έχω	⊙	τρεις κόρες
	⊙	δύο παιδιά
	⊙	ένα παιδί

Listen and speak

TRACK NUMBER
38

Now imagine you are with some of your family looking for the station and you meet a Greek friend, Pavlos.

Prepare carefully the information you need below to take part in the conversation. Then go to your audio CD and see how you get on introducing your family.

1 Think of two members of your family – one male and one female. For example, your husband and your daughter; or your brother and your mother.

2 How would you introduce them to Pavlos in Greek?

3 How would you ask *How do I get to the station?*

4 How do you say *thank you* and *goodbye*?

You can repeat the conversation, but this time use two different members of your family and ask how to get to the bus stop.

TOPIC 7: Who's this?

Bingo!

1. Cut out the small number tokens and the bingo cards on Game Card 7.

2. Find 16 buttons for each player or make 16 small blank pieces of card (to cover the squares on the bingo card).

3. Put the tokens into a bag and shake thoroughly.

4. Pull out a number token and say the number out loud in Greek.

5. If you have that number on your card, cover the square with a button or blank piece of card. If you have more than one square with that number, you can only cover one.

6. Put the number token back in the bag and shake again.

7. Repeat steps 3–6 until you have all the squares covered on the bingo card. Then you can shout: Νίκησα! **níkisa** (*I've won!*)

You can play with a friend or challenge yourself.

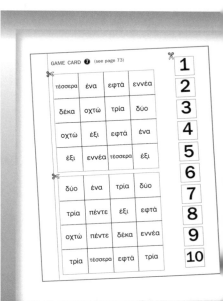

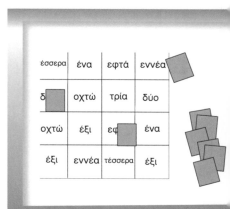

Key Words

TRACK NUMBER
39

γιατρός **yiatrós**	doctor	μάγειρας **máyiras**	cook/chef
		(fem. μαγείρισσα **mayírisa**)	
υπάλληλος **ipálilos**	employee		
		λογιστής **loyistís**	accountant
οδηγός **οτηigós**	driver	(fem. λογίστρια **loyístria**)	
μηχανικός **mihanikós**	engineer	δάσκαλος **τηáskalos**	teacher
		(fem. δασκάλα **τηáskala**)	
ηθοποιός **ithopiós**	actor		
		φοιτητής **fititís**	student
δικηγόρος **τηikigóros**	lawyer	(fem. φοιτήτρια **fitítria**)	

Notice that some jobs have a different ending for the feminine, but others use the same word for both males and females.

If your job or those of your family aren't listed here, try to find out what they are in Greek.

TOPIC 8: What do you do?

What does it mean?

Join the Greek to the pronunciation and the English, as in the example.

δάσκαλος	οτηigós	employee
φοιτητής	ithopiós	accountant
γιατρός	τηikigóros	actor
μάγειρας	yiatrós	driver
υπάλληλος	máyiras	lawyer
μηχανικός	τηáskalos	engineer
λογιστής	fititís	doctor
οδηγός	ipálilos	cook/chef
ηθοποιός	mihanikós	teacher
δικηγόρος	loyistís	student

The tools of the trade

Match the jobs to the tools of the trade, as in the example.

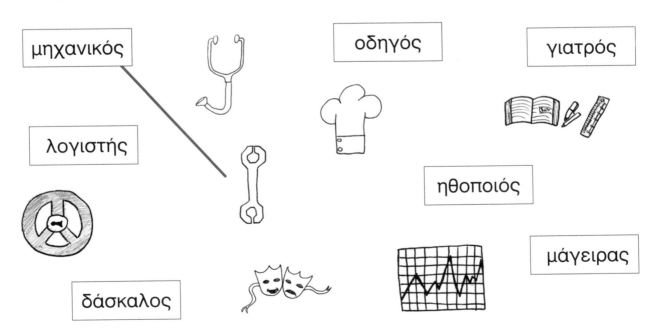

μηχανικός

λογιστής

δάσκαλος

οδηγός

ηθοποιός

γιατρός

μάγειρας

Language Focus

◎ ◎ ◎ ◎ ◎ To ask what someone does for a living, you use the phrase: Τι δουλειά κάνετε; **ti тноoliá kánete** *What work do you do?*

◎ ◎ ◎ ◎ You will have noticed on page 75 that some professions have a different male and female form of the word, and the answer will vary accordingly:

> Τι δουλειά κάνετε; **ti тноoliá kánete?**
> *What work do you do?*
>
> Είμαι γιατρός. **íme yiatrós** *I am [a] doctor.* (male or female)
>
> Τι δουλειά κάνετε; **ti тноuliá kánete?**
> *What work do you do?*
>
> Είμαι μάγειρας. **íme máyiras** *I am [a] cook.* (male)
>
> Τι δουλειά κάνετε; **ti тноuliá kánete?**
> *What work do you do?*
>
> Είμαι δασκάλα. **íme тнaskála** *I am [a] teacher.* (female)

Notice that you do not need the word for "a" in Greek in this expression.

◎ ◎ ◎ Other possible answers include:

> Είμαι συνταξιούχος.
> **íme sindaksioóhos**
> *I'm retired.*
>
> Δεν δουλεύω τώρα.
> **тнen тноolévo tóra**

Listen and note

TRACK NUMBER
40

Listen to two people telling you about themselves
and fill out the details in English on the forms below.

First name: .....Maria..........................

Family name:.....................................

Nationality: ....

Name of spouse: ....

No. of children: ....

Occupation: ....

First name: ....

Family name:.....................................

Nationality: ....

Name of spouse: ....

No. of children: ....

Occupation: ....

Your turn to speak

TRACK NUMBER
41

Now you give same information about yourself.
Follow the prompts on your audio CD.

What's the answer?

Match the questions to the answers.

For example: 1d

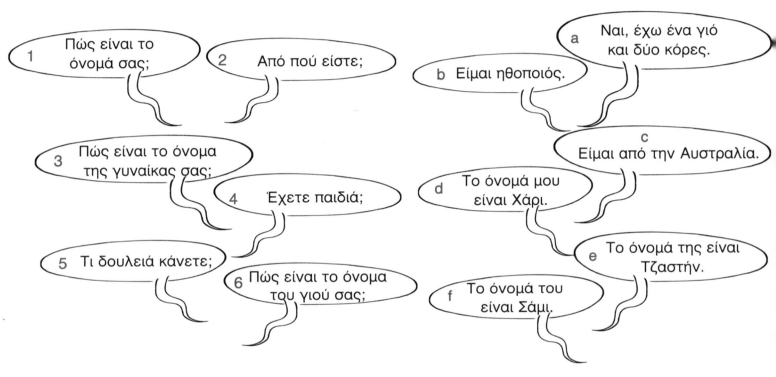

1 Πώς είναι το όνομά σας;

2 Από πού είστε;

3 Πώς είναι το όνομα της γυναίκας σας;

4 Έχετε παιδιά;

5 Τι δουλειά κάνετε;

6 Πώς είναι το όνομα του γιού σας;

a Ναι, έχω ένα γιό και δύο κόρες.

b Είμαι ηθοποιός.

c Είμαι από την Αυστραλία.

d Το όνομά μου είναι Χάρι.

e Το όνομά της είναι Τζαστήν.

f Το όνομά του είναι Σάμι.

Which word?

Write the correct number of the word in the box to complete the description, as in the example.

1 γυναίκας	2 γιό
3 ηθοποιός	4 κόρες
5 παιδιά	

Το όνομά μου είναι Χάρι και είμαι

___3___ . Είμαι από την Μελβούρνη

στην Αυστραλία. Το όνομα της

_____ μου είναι Τζαστήν, και έχω

τρία _____ – ένα _____ και

δύο _____ .

TOPIC 8: What do you do?

Key Words

το εργοστάσιο *factory*
ergostásio (pl. εργοστάσια)

το γραφείο *office*
grafío (pl. γραφεία)

το κατάστημα *store*
katastima (pl. καταστήματα)

το πανεπιστήμιο *university*
panepistímio (pl. πανεπιστήμια)

το θέατρο *theater*
théatro (pl. θέατρα)

η εταιρία *company/*
etería (pl. εταιρίες) *business*

See page 54 for more places to work.

Language Focus

To answer the question Πού δουλεύετε; **poo τΗoolévete** *Where do you work?* you can use the phrase Δουλεύω σε ... **τΗoolévo se ...** *I work in ...* :

Είμαι γιατρός και δουλεύω σε ένα μικρό νοσοκομείο στην Θεσσαλονίκη.**íme yiatrós ke τΗoolévo se éna mikró nosokomío stin Thesaloníki**
I am a doctor and I work in a small hospital in Thessaloniki.

Δουλεύω σε μία μεγάλη εταιρία στην Αθήνα.
τΗoolévo se mía megáli etería stin athína
I work in a large company in Athens.

Where do I work?

Can you match the work places to the jobs as in the example?

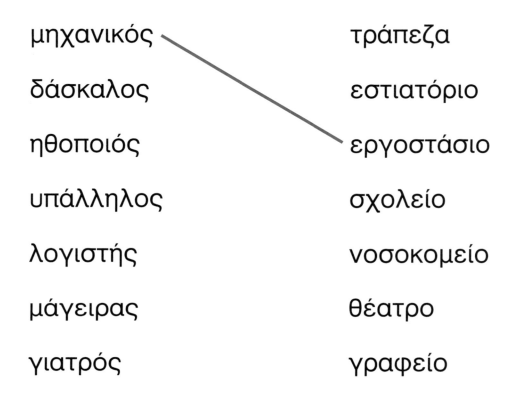

μηχανικός	τράπεζα
δάσκαλος	εστιατόριο
ηθοποιός	εργοστάσιο
υπάλληλος	σχολείο
λογιστής	νοσοκομείο
μάγειρας	θέατρο
γιατρός	γραφείο

Now make sentences for each of the work-places, for example:

Είμαι μηχανικός και δουλεύω σε ένα εργοστάσιο.

íme mihanikós ke ΤΗοolévo se éna ergostásio

I'm an engineer and I work in a factory.

What are they saying?

Match the people with what they are saying. For example: 1e

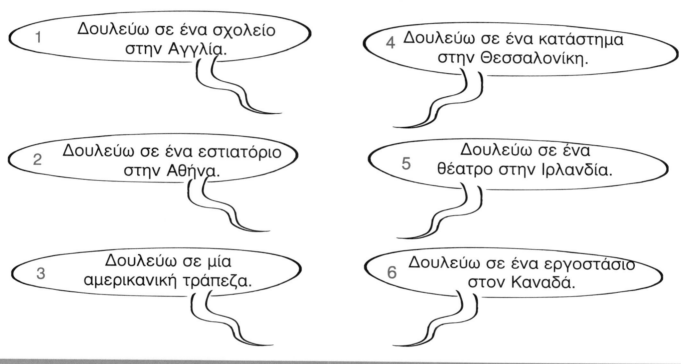

1　Δουλεύω σε ένα σχολείο στην Αγγλία.

2　Δουλεύω σε ένα εστιατόριο στην Αθήνα.

3　Δουλεύω σε μία αμερικανική τράπεζα.

4　Δουλεύω σε ένα κατάστημα στην Θεσσαλονίκη.

5　Δουλεύω σε ένα θέατρο στην Ιρλανδία.

6　Δουλεύω σε ένα εργοστάσιο στον Καναδά.

a

b

c

d

e

f

Listen and speak

TRACK NUMBER
43

Imagine you are a Greek chef. You're meeting someone for the first time and they are asking you about yourself.

Prepare carefully the information below you will need to take part in the conversation. Then go to your audio CD and see how you get on talking about yourself.

1 Your name is Giannis Leonidas (Γιάννης Λεωνίδας).

2 You're from Athens, Greece but you work in America.

3 You're a chef.

4 You work in a Greek restaurant in New York.

5 You have two daughters.

6 Your wife is a teacher in a big school.

Which word?

Now write the correct number of the word in the box to complete the description of Giannis's life, as in the example.

1 ελληνικό	2 πανεπιστήμιο	3 μάγειρας	4 εστιατόριο
5 δασκάλα	6 φοιτήτριες	7 σχολείο	8 δουλεύω

Το όνομά μου είναι Γιάννης Λεωνίδας. Είμαι ___3___ . Είμαι από την Αθήνα

στην Ελλάδα, αλλά _____ σε ένα _____ _____ στην Νέα Υόρκη. Η

γυναίκα μου είναι _____ και δουλεύει σε ένα μεγάλο _____ κοντά στο

εστιατόριο. Έχουμε δύο κόρες και είναι _____ στο _____ .

Where do I work?

(1) Tear out the work-place picture cards and profession word cards on Game Card 8.

(2) Turn the cards face down on a table, with the pictures on one end of the table and the words on the other.

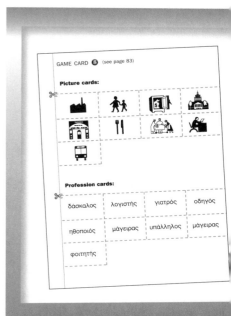

(3) Turn a word card and say Είμαι... **íme...**, not forgetting to add the feminine ending if you are female e.g. Είμαι δάσκαλος/δασκάλα. **íme THáskalos/THaskála** (*I'm a teacher.*)

(4) Then turn a picture card. If the work-place picture matches the profession, say Δουλεύω σε ένα/μία ... **THoolévo se éna/mía ...** e.g. Δουλεύω σε ένα σχολείο. **THoolévo se éna skolío** (*I work in a school*).

(5) If you turn a matching picture and say both sentences correctly, you get to keep the cards. If you don't, you must turn the cards face down and try again.

(6) The winner is the one who collects the most cards.

(7) You can compete with a friend or challenge yourself against the clock.

(Review the vocabulary on pages 54, 56 and 74 before you play the game.)

This **Test Yourself** section reviews all the Greek you have learned in this programme. Have a go at the activities. If you find you have forgotten something, go back to the relevant topic(s) and look again at the **Key Words** and **Language Focus** panels.

I want..., please.

Ask for the following, as in the example:

 Θέλω ένα τσάϊ, παρακαλώ.
thélo ena tsai, parakaló

1

4

2

5

3

Listen and tick

Listen to Katerina talking about herself and decide if the following sentences are true or false.

TRACK NUMBER **44**

		True	False
1	Katerina is Greek.	☐	☐
2	She comes from a small town.	☐	☐
3	She's a teacher.	☐	☐
4	She works in England.	☐	☐
5	Her husband is an engineer.	☐	☐
6	She has five children.	☐	☐

Which word?

Now write the correct number of the word in the box to complete the description of Katerina, as in the example.

1 δίπλα	2 γιό	3 ελληνικό	4 τέσσερα
5 νοσοκομείο	6 πόλη	7 γιατρός	8 Ελλάδα

Το όνομά μου είναι Κατερίνα, και είμαι από την Θεσσαλονίκη, μία μεγάλη

__6__ στην ____ . Είμαι δασκάλα, και δουλεύω σε ένα μικρό ____ σχολείο

στην Αγγλία. Ο άντρας μου είναι ____ , και δουλεύει σε ένα μεγάλο ____

____ στο ελληνικό σχολείο. Έχουμε ____ παιδιά, ένα ____ και τρεις κόρες.

Can you try and make up a similar description about yourself?

Read and tick

Look at the picture and decide if the sentences are true or false. Look back at topics 4–6 if you are unsure of any of the words. *(Note: to work out "left" and "right", imagine you have your <u>back</u> to the buildings, facing away.)*

		True	False
1	Υπάρχει μία τράπεζα στο κάδρο.	❏	❏
2	Υπάρχει ένα νοσοκομείο δίπλα στην τράπεζα δεξιά.	❏	❏
3	Υπάρχει ένα σχολείο δίπλα στην τράπεζα αριστερά.	❏	❏
4	Υπάρχει ένας σκύλος στο δρόμο.	❏	❏
5	Δεν υπάρχουν αυτοκίνητα στο δρόμο.	❏	❏
6	Υπάρχει μία μικρή γάτα πάνω από το αυτοκίνητο.	❏	❏
7	Υπάρχουν μεγάλα δέντρα πίσω από το σχολείο.	❏	❏
8	Υπάρχει ένα παλιό ποδήλατο μπροστά από το νοσοκομείο.	❏	❏

What does it mean?

Can you remember these words? Join the words and write the pronunciation next to the Greek, as in the example

children	γιός	_yiós_
husband	αδελφός	
son	γιοί	
daughter	κόρες	
father	παιδί	
mother	μητέρα	
brother	αδελφή	
daughters	γυναίκα	
child	αδελφοί	
wife	παιδιά	
sister	άντρας	
brothers	αδελφές	
sons	κόρη	
sisters	πατέρας	

How do you say it?

Now see if you can say these in Greek, as in the example.

1 **My husband is a doctor.**
Ο άντρας μου είναι γιατρός.
o ándras moo íne yiatrós

2 I have four children.

3 Our son is an engineer.

4 Maria's mother is from Athens.

5 My wife's name is Claire.

6 My brother is an actor.

7 I don't have any sisters.

8 I have three daughters.

At the tourist information office

TRACK NUMBER 45

Finally, you are going to test your new Greek conversational skills by joining in the dialogue on your audio CD.

You're going to ask for some information at a tourist information office.

To prepare, first see if you can remember these words and phrases. Write the pronunciation and English next to the Greek, as in the example.

αντίο	**adío**	_goodbye_
ευχαριστώ		
πίσω από		
δεξιά		
αριστερά		
δρόμος		
λεωφορείο		
κοντά		
μεγάλος/-η/-ο		
μουσείο		
πού		
καλημέρα		

Now follow the prompts on your audio CD. Don't worry if you don't manage everything the first time around. Just keep repeating it until you are fluent.

Congratulations on successfully completing this introductory *Read and Speak Greek for Beginners* programme. You have overcome the obstacle of learning a new language in an unfamiliar script. You should now have the confidence to enjoy using the Greek you have learned. You have also acquired a sound basis from which to expand your language skills in whichever direction you choose. Good luck!

This **Reference** section gives an overview of the Greek script and pronunciation. You can use it to refer to as you work your way through the *Read and Speak Greek for Beginners* programme. Don't expect to take it all in from the beginning. The programme is designed to build your confidence step by step as you progress through the topics. The details will start to fall into place gradually as you become more familiar with the Greek letters and language.

The Greek script

The Greek script is not nearly as difficult as it might seem at first glance. There are many letters that are the same as the English ones, there are capital letters, and, unlike English, words are usually spelled as they sound.

There are 24 letters altogether in the Greek alphabet. A good way of remembering the alphabet is to divide the letters into three groups.

The first group consists of ten letters which look and sound like their English equivalents. Eight are very similar – but watch out for lower case Z (ζ) and M (μ):

Capital letter:	A	E	Z	I	K	M	O	T
Lower case:	α	ε	ζ	ι	κ	μ	o	τ
Pronunciation:	**a**	**e**	**z**	**i**	**k**	**m**	**o**	**t**

The other letters in this group can be misleading. The Greek N **n** is pronounced the same as English but in lower case looks like an English 'v'. Likewise the Greek Y **i** looks like an English 'u' in lower case (see also page 91 for pronunciation):

Capital letter:	N	Y
Lower case:	ν	υ
Pronunciation:	**n**	**i**

The second group of letters resemble English letters as capitals, but they represent totally different sounds. These are called "false friends".

Capital letter:	B	H	P	X
Lower case:	β	η	ρ	χ
Pronunciation:	**v**	**i**	**r**	**h** *(hard)*

○ ○ ○ The third group consists of the remaining nine letters that have unfamiliar shapes, although most of them represent sounds familiar to an English-speaker. The first four shown below represent sounds that in English are made by putting two letters together. Some of these letters may look familiar through their use in mathematics and science.

Capital letter:	Δ	Θ	Ξ	Ψ	Φ	Λ	Π	Σ	Ω
Lower case:	δ	θ	ξ	ψ	φ	λ	π	σ, ς*	ω
Pronunciation:	TH	th	ks	ps	f	l	p	s	o

* The form of this letter depends on its position in a word. ς is only used at the end of a word, otherwise σ is used, e.g. σκύλος (**skilos**) – dog.

The Greek alphabet

The table below shows all the Greek letters, both capitals and lower case, in alphabetical order with their pronunciation. You can refer to it as you work your way through the topics.

A	α	**a**	I	ι	**i**	P	ρ	**r**
B	β	**v**	K	κ	**k**	Σ	σ ς	**s**
Γ	γ	**gh/y**	Λ	λ	**l**	T	τ	**t**
Δ	δ	**TH** (as in "<u>that</u>")	M	μ	**m**	Y	υ	**i**
E	ε	**e**	N	ν	**n**	Φ	φ	**f**
Z	ζ	**z**	Ξ	ξ	**ks**	X	χ	**h**
H	η	**i**	O	o	**o**	Ψ	ψ	**ps**
Θ	θ	**th** (as in "<u>thin</u>")	Π	π	**p**	Ω	ω	**o**

Pronunciation

⊙ ⊙ ⊙ ⊙ Greek is probably one of the easiest languages to read as what you see is generally what you hear. The Greek used today is very much simplified. The once prolific stress and breathing marks have been reduced to only one small accent above a vowel (e.g. ó) which indicates where the stress falls on a word.

⊙ ⊙ ⊙ ⊙ The Greek vowels have simple pronunciations:

A, α	always pronounced "a" as in "bat"
E, ε	always pronounced "e" as in "bed"
I, ι / Y, υ / H, η	all pronounced "ee" as in "feet"
O, o / Ω, ω	both pronounced "o" as in "pot"

⊙ ⊙ ⊙ A combination of two vowels may produce a different sound. Use the pronunciation guide for individual words to help you. Note these especially:

αυ	pronounced "af" or "av", e.g. αυτοκίνητο (**aftokinito**) – "car"; Παύλος (**Pavlos**)
ευ	pronounced "ef" or "ev", e.g. ευχαριστώ (**efharisto**) – "thank you"

⊙ ⊙ Many of the other Greek letters are pronounced in a similar way to their English equivalents, but here are a few points to note:

P, ρ (**r**)	pronounced trilled as the Scottish "r" at of the front of the mouth
X, χ (**h**)	pronounced like the "ch" in the Yiddish "chutzpah"
Γ, γ (**gh/y**)	pronounced like a softer "g", except when it is followed by an **i** or **e** sound, when it is pronounced as "y" in the English "yes".

You will find an introduction to the sounds of Greek on track 1 of your audio.

Topic 1

Page 6
Check your answers with the Key Words panel on page 5.

Page 8: What are they saying?

Page 8: What do you hear?
You should have ticked boxes 2 and 5.

Page 10: What does it mean?
1d, 2f, 3e, 4a, 5b, 6c

Page 10: Which word?
Καλη __2__ .
Γειά σας, __5__ σπέρα.
Το __4__ μου __6__ Άννα.
Πως είναι το όνομά __3__ ;
Το όνομά __1__ είναι Γιώργος.

Page 11: What are their names?

Κάθριν	Catherine	Τζων	John
Μαίρη	Mary	Ντέιβιντ	David
Αvv	Ann	Μάικλ	Michael
Ελίζαμπεθ	Elizabeth	Χάρρυ	Harry

Page 12: In or out?
IN: Elizabeth, John, Catherine, Harry, David
OUT: Anna, Kostas, Michael, Yiorgos, Mary

Topic 2

Page 15: Where are the countries?

ο Καναδάς __1__ η Ελλάδα __6__ η Αγγλία __4__ η Ιταλία __5__

η Ιρλανδία __3__ η Αμερική __2__ η Τουρκία __7__ η Αυστραλία __8__

Page 16: How do you say it?
Check your answers with the Key Words panel on page 14.

Page 16: Where are the cities?
Η Αθήνα είναι στην Ελλάδα. **i athína íne stin elátha**

Η Νέα Υόρκη είναι στην Αμερική. **i nea yórki íne stin amerikí**

Η Ουάσινγκτον είναι στην Αμερική. **i ouásington íne stin amerikí**

Η Άγκυρα είναι στην Τουρκία. **i ángira íne stin tourkía**

Η Θεσσαλονίκη είναι στην Ελλάδα. **i thessaloníki íne stin elátha**

Το Σίντνεϊ είναι στην Αυστραλία. **to sídnei íne stin avstralía**

Το Λονδίνο είναι στην Αγγλία. **to lonthíno íne stin anglía**

Το Δουβλίνο είναι στην Ιρλανδία. **to doovlíno íne stin irlanthía**

Page 17: Audio track 8
Maria: Greece; Michael America; Susan: England; Selim: Turkey; Nicoletta: Italy; Stuart: Canada

Page 18: Where are they from?

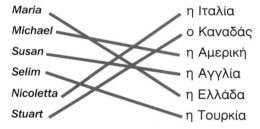

Page 20: Who's from where?
1 Αυτός είναι από την Νέα Υόρκη, στην Αμερική.
aftós íne apó tin néa yórki, stin amerikí.
2 Αυτή είναι από την Αθήνα, στην Ελλάδα.
aftí íne apó tin athína stin elátha
3 Αυτή είναι από το Βανκούβερ, στον Καναδά.
aftí íne apó to vankoúver, ston kanathá
4 Αυτός είναι από το Σίντνεϊ, στην Αυστραλία.
aftós íne apó to sídnei, stin afstralía
5 Αυτός είναι από το Δουβλίνο, στην Ιρλανδία.
aftós íne apó to THouvlíno, stin irlanTHía
6 Αυτή είναι από την Ρώμη, στην Ιταλία.
aftí íne apó tin rómi, stin italía

7 Αυτός είναι από την Αγκύρα, στην Τουρκία.
   aftós íne apó tin angíra, stin tourkía

8 Αυτή είναι από το Λονδίνο, στην Αγγλία.
   aftí íne apó to lonTHíno, stin anglía

Page 21: Listen and tick

1 False; 2 True; 3 False; 4 True; 5 False

Page 21: What does it mean?

I'm from Canada.   Το όνομά μου είναι Λούσυ.

He's from Greece.   Εγώ είμαι από τον Καναδά.

My name's Lucy.   Γειά σας.

What's your name?   Πώς είναι το όνομά σας;

Good evening.   Αυτός είναι από την Ελλάδα.

Hello.   Καλησπέρα.

Page 22: What does it mean?

1 Το όνομά μου είναι Λούσυ.   My name is Lucy.
2 Είμαι από τον Καναδά.   I'm from Canada.
3 Ο Κώστας είναι από την Ελλάδα. Kostas is from Greece.
4 Πώς είναι το όνομά σας;   What's your name?
5 Το όνομά μου είναι Μαρία.   My name is Maria.
6 Από πού είναι αυτός;   Where is he from?
7 Αυτός είναι από την Αγγλία.   He's from England.
8 Αυτή είναι από την Αμερική.   She's from America.

Topic 3

Page 25

Check your answers with the Key Words panel on page 24.

Page 26:
Word Square

sofa, table, book, door, chair, telephone, bag

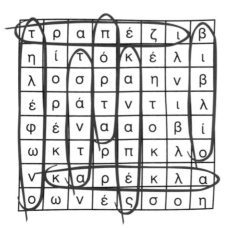

Page 26: Odd One Out

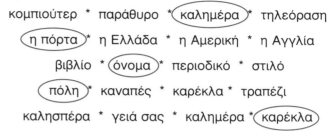

κομπιούτερ * παράθυρο * (καλημέρα) * τηλεόραση

(η πόρτα) * η Ελλάδα * η Αμερική * η Αγγλία

βιβλίο * (όνομα) * περιοδικό * στιλό

(πόλη) * καναπές * καρέκλα * τραπέζι

καλησπέρα * γειά σας * καλημέρα * (καρέκλα)

Page 28: What is it?

1e, 2b, 3f, 4c, 5h, 6d, 7a, 8g

Page 30: Who orders what?

Customer 1: coffee & sandwich; Customer 2: coffee & cake; Customer 3: coffee & sweet; Customer 4: tea, cake & ice cream; Customer 5: tea, coffee and cheese pie

Page 31: Unscramble the conversation

g, a, e, c, f, h, d, b

Topic 4

Page 35: What does it mean?

Check your answers with the Key Words panel on page 34.

Page 35: What can you see?

γάτα ☑	ψυγείο ☐
σκύλος ☐	παράθυρο ☑
φούρνος ☐	κρεβάτι ☑
τραπέζι ☑	κουρτίνα ☑
στιλό ☑	ποντίκι ☐
βιβλίο ☑	πόρτα ☐
περιοδικό ☐	κάδρο ☑
κομπιούτερ ☑	ντουλάπι ☐
τσάντα ☑	καρέκλα ☑

Page 37: Which word?

1 μπροστά από; 2 κάτω από; 3 πάνω από; 4 σ(ε);
5 κάτω από; 6 δίπλα σ(ε); 7 μέσα σ(ε)

Page 39: Where are the mice

There are many possible sentences.
If you can, check yours with a native speaker.

Page 41: True or False?

1 True; 2 False; 3 False; 4 False; 5 False; 6 True; 7 False;
8 True; 9 True; 10 True

Topic 5

Page 44: Can you remember?

Check your answers with the Key Words panel.

Page 46: What does it mean?

ένα μεγάλο σάντουϊτς *a big sandwich*

ένα μικρό ποντίκι *a small mouse*

ένας μικρός σκύλος *a small dog*

ένας καινούριος καναπές *a new sofa*

ένα μεγάλο δέντρο *a big tree*

ένα πολύ παλιό αυτοκίνητο *a very old car*

ένα φτηνό κάδρο *an inexpensive picture*

ένας μικρός καφές *a small coffee*

Page 47: Listen and tick

1 False; 2 True; 3 True; 4 False; 5 True

Page 47: Unscramble the sentences

1: 3, 1, 2;   2: 2, 3, 1, 5, 4;   3: 1, 3, 2;
4: 1, 3, 5, 2, 4   5: 1, 4, 3, 2

Page 50: Which word?

1 κεφάλι; 2 πόδι; 3 στομάχι; 4 στόμα; 5 ουρά;
6 μαλλιά; 7 αυτιά; 8 μύτη; 9 μάτια; 10 χέρι

Page 51: At the circus

Ο Κάρλος έχει ___6___ μάτια και ένα ___1___ στομάχι.

Έχει μια ___4___ τσάντα στο χέρι.

Η Καρλόττα έχει μια ___2___ μύτη και ένα ___5___ στόμα.

Έχει μια ___3___ γάτα.

Page 52: What does it look like?

There are many possible sentences.
If you can, check yours with a native speaker.

Topic 6

Page 55: Questions and answers

Πού είναι η τράπεζα;

Υπάρχει ένα εστιατόριο;

Υπάρχει ένα ξενοδοχείο;

Πού είναι το νοσοκομείο;

Πού είναι η γέφυρα;

Το νοσοκομείο είναι κοντά στο σχολείο.

Υπάρχει ένα ξενοδοχείο μπροστά από το σταθμό.

Ναι, υπάρχει ένα εστιατόριο.

Η γέφυρα είναι εκεί.

Η τράπεζα είναι δίπλα στο σχολείο.

Page 57: Word Square

taxi, bus, plane, car, train, bicycle, boat

α	λ	υ	κ	η	τx	υ	ν	α
κ	ε	τ	α	μ	σ	η	α	υ
υ	ω	τ	α	ξ	ί	σ	ε	τ
η	φ	ρ	ξ	ρ	ε	δ	ρ	ο
π	ο	δ	ή	λ	α	τ	ο	κ
ό	ρ	ν	ε	ι	τ	α	π	ί
δ	ε	ο	η	κ	ρ	ε	λ	ν
ι	ί	α	σ	λ	έ	τ	ά	η
τ	ο	η	υ	α	ν	ρ	ν	τ
λ	ε	ω	π	λ	ο	ί	ο	ι

Page 60: Which way?

1 Συγνώμη. Πώς πάω στην στάση; Ευθεία.
   signómi. pos pao stin stási? efthía

2 Συγνώμη. Πώς πάω στο νοσοκομίο; Πάρτε τον πρώτο
   δρόμο δεξιά. **signómi. pos pao sto nosokomío? párte ton
   próto тнrómo deksiá**

3 Συγνώμη. Πώς πάω στην τράπεζα; Πάρτε τον πρώτο
   δρόμο αριστερά. **signómi. pos pao stin trápeza? párte ton
   próto тнrómo aristerá**

4 Συγνώμη. Πώς πάω στο ξενοδοχείο; Πάρτε τον
   δεύτερο δρόμο δεξιά. **signómi. pos pao sto ksenoтнohío?
   párte ton тнeftero тнrómo aristerá**

5 Συγνώμη. Πώς πάω στο μουσείο; Με το λεωφορείο.
   signómi. pos pao sto mousío? me to leoforío

6 Συγνώμη. Πώς πάω στο αεροδρόμιο; Με το τρένο.
   signómi. pos pao sto aeroтнrómio? me to tréno

Page 61: Around town

These are model answers. Yours may vary slightly.

Hotel Byron: Για το ξενοδοχείο Βύρωνας, πηγαίνετε ευθεία από εδώ. Είναι δεξιά, μετά από τον πρώτο δρόμο.

yia to ksenoτноhío Víronas, piyénete efthía apo ethó. íne τнeksiá metá apó ton próto τнrómo

Park: Για το πάρκο, πηγαίνετε ευθεία από εδώ, πάρτε τον πρώτο δρόμο αριστερά. Είναι δίπλα στο σχολείο.

yia to párko, piyénete efthía apo ετнó, párte ton próto τнrómo aristerá. íne τнípla sto sxolío

Bus stop: Για την στάση, πηγαίνετε ευθεία από εδώ, πάρτε τον πρώτο δρόμο αριστερά. Είναι απέναντι από το σχολείο.

yia tin stási, piyénete efthía apo ετнó, párte ton próto τнrómo aristerá. íne apentandi apó to sxolío

Page 62: Unscramble the conversation

f, g, d, c, a, b, e

Page 63: Game

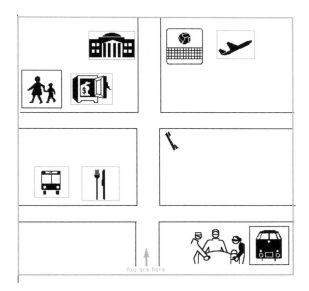

Topic 7

Page 65: What does it mean?

Check your answers with the Key Words panel on page 64.

Page 67: Family Tree

There are many possible sentences.
If you can, check yours with a native speaker.

Page 68: Giorgos's family

Παύλος
Κώστας
Γιώργος

Αντρέας
Ελένη
Μαρία

Γιώργος
Κώστας
Χάρρυ

Γιάννης
Παύλος
Κώστας

Page 68: Questions and answers

1 Έχεις αδελφούς;
2 Πώς είναι το όνομα της μητέρας σου;
3 Έχεις αδελφές;
4 Πώς είναι το όνομα του αδελφού σου;
5 Πώς είναι το όνομα του πατέρα σου;
6 Πώς είναι το όνομά σου;
7 Από πού είσαι;

a Το όνομά της είναι Μαρία.
b Όχι. Δεν έχω αδελφές.
c Το όνομά του είναι Κώστας.
d Είμαι από την Χαλκίδα.
e Το όνομά μου είναι Γιώργος.
f Το όνομά του είναι Παύλος.
g Ναι. Έχω έναν αδελφό

Page 71: How many?

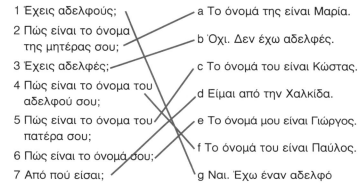

οχτώ
τέσσερα
πέντε
εφτά
έξι
τρία
δύο
εννέα
ένα
δέκα

téssera
pénde
éksi
éna
enéa
théka
eftá
októ
thío
tría

Page 71: Greek sums

1 τέσσερα; 2 οχτώ; 3 τρία; 4 εννέα; 5 εφτά;
6 έξι; 7 δέκα; 8 εννέα; 9 δέκα

Page 72: My family

There are many possible sentences.
If you can, check yours with a native speaker.

Topic 8

Page 75: What does it mean?
Check your answers with the Key Words panel on page 74.

Page 75: The tools of the trade

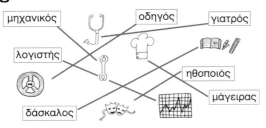

μηχανικός
οδηγός
γιατρός
λογιστής
ηθοποιός
μάγειρας
δάσκαλος

Page 77: Listen and note
1 *First name:* Maria; *Family name:* Vazaka; *Nationality:* Greek; *Spouse:* Yiorgos; *Children:* 2; *Occupation:* accountant

2 *First name:* Piero; *Family name:* Andreotti; *Nationality:* Italian; *Spouse:* Anna; *Children:* 3; *Occupation:* engineer

Page 78: What does it mean?
1d, 2c, 3e, 4a, 5b, 6f

Page 78: Which word?
Το όνομά μου είναι Χάρι και είμαι __3__ . Είμαι από την Μελβούρνη στην Αυστραλία. Το όνομα της __1__ μου είναι Τζαστήν, και έχω τρία __5__ – ένα __2__ και δύο __4__ .

Page 80: Where do I work?

μηχανικός — τράπεζα
δάσκαλος — εστιατόριο
ηθοποιός — εργοστάσιο
υπάλληλος — σχολείο
λογιστής — νοσοκομείο
μάγειρας — θέατρο
γιατρός — γραφείο

Page 81: What are they saying?
1d, 2e, 3b, 4c, 5a, 6f

Page 82: Which word?
Το όνομά μου είναι Γιάννης Λεωνίδας. Είμαι __3__ . Είμαι από την Αθήνα στην Ελλάδα, αλλά __8__ σε ένα __1__ __4__ στην Νέα Υόρκη. Η γυναίκα μου είναι __5__ και δουλεύει σε ένα μεγάλο __7__ κοντά στο εστιατόριο. Έχουμε δύο κόρες και είναι __6__ στο __2__ .

Test Yourself

Page 84: I want …, please?
1 Θέλω έναν καφέ, παρακαλώ. **thélo énan kafé, parakaló**
2 Θέλω ένα κεϊκ, παρακαλώ. **thélo éna keik, parakaló**
3 Θέλω μια τυρόπιττα, παρακαλώ. **thélo mia tirópitta, parakaló**
4 Θέλω ένα παγωτό, παρακαλώ. **thélo éna pagotó, parakaló**
5 Θέλω ένα σάντουϊτς, παρακαλώ. **thélo éna sándouits, parakaló**

Page 85: Listen and tick
1 True; 2 False; 3 True; 4 True; 5 False; 6 False

Page 85: Which word?
Το όνομά μου είναι Κατερίνα, και είμαι από την Θεσσαλονίκη, μία μεγάλη __6__ στην __8__ . Είμαι δασκάλα, και δουλεύω σε ένα μικρό __3__ σχολείο στην Αγγλία. Ο άντρας μου είναι __7__ , και δουλεύει σε ένα μεγάλο __5__ __1__ στο ελληνικό σχολείο. Έχουμε __4__ παιδιά, ένα __2__ και τρεις κόρες.

Page 86: Read and tick
1 True; 2 True; 3 False; 4 True; 5 False; 6 True; 7 True; 8 False

Page 87: Read and tick
Check your answers with the Key Words panel on page 64.

Page 87: How do you say it?
1 Ο άντρας μου είναι γιατρός. **o ándras moo íne yiatrós**
2 Έχω τέσσερα παιδιά. **ého téssera peтнiá**
3 Ο γιός μας είναι μηχανικός. **o yios mas íne mihanikos**
4 Η μητέρα της Μαρίας είναι από την Αθήνα. **i mitéra tis marias íne apó tin athína**
5 Το όνομα της γυναίκας μου είναι Κλαιρ. **to ónoma tis yinékas mou íne klair**
6 Ο αδελφός μου είναι ηθοποιός. **o aтнelfós mou íne ithopiós**
7 Δεν έχω αδελφές. **then ého aтнelfés**
8 Έχω τρεις κόρες. **ého tris kóres**

Page 88: At the tourist office

αντίο	**adío**	*goodbye*
ευχαριστώ	**efharistó**	*thank you*
πίσω από	**píso apó**	*behind*
δεξιά	**deksiá**	*right*
αριστερά	**aristerá**	*left*
δρόμος	**тнrómos**	*street*
λεωφορείο	**leoforío**	*bus*
κοντά	**kontá**	*near*
μεγάλος/-η/-ο	**megálos/-i/-o**	*goodbye*
μουσείο	**moosío**	*museum*
πού	**poo**	*where*
καλημέρα	**kaliméra**	*good morning*

Name cards:

Γιώργο(ς)	Άννα	Κώστα(ς)	Μαρία
Ελίζαμπεθ	Ανν	Μαίρη	Κάθριν
Χάρρυ	Μάικλ	Ντέιβιντ	Τζων

Sentence-build cards:

;	το όνομά μου	κύριε	είναι
.	το όνομά σου	ευχαριστώ	καλημέρα
αντίο	το όνομά σας	παρακαλώ	καλησπέρα
πώς	κυρία	γειά σας	γειά σου

Maria	Kostas	Anna	Yiorgo(s)
Catherine	Mary	Ann	Elizabeth
John	David	Michael	Harry

is	Mr	my name	?
good morning	thank you	your name *(informal)*	.
good evening	please	your name *(polite)*	goodbye
hello *(informal)*	hello *(polite)*	Mrs	what

GAME CARD ❸ (see page 33)

Picture cards:

Cut-out pictures (cut round small pictures)

  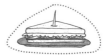

Sentence-build cards:

πάνω από τον	δίπλα στον	κάτω από τον	στον
πάνω από το	δίπλα στο	κάτω από το	στο
πάνω από την	δίπλα στην	κάτω από την	στην
καναπές	κρεβάτι	τραπέζι	καρέκλα
ένα σάντουϊτς	ένα κάδρο	ένα τηλέφωνο	ένα κομπιούτερ
Υπάρχει	μία γάτα	ένα ποντίκι	μία τηλεόραση

in/on the *(masculine)*	**under the** *(masculine)*	**next to the** *(masculine)*	**above the** *(masculine)*
in/on the *(neuter)*	**under the** *(neuter)*	**next to the** *(neuter)*	**above the** *(neuter)*
in/on the *(feminine)*	**under the** *(feminine)*	**next to the** *(feminine)*	**above the** *(feminine)*
chair	**table**	**bed**	**sofa**
a computer	**a telephone**	**a picture**	**a sandwich**
a television	**a mouse**	**a cat**	**There's**

Picture cards:

Adjective cards:

μεγάλος	μικρός	καινούριος	παλιός
ακριβός	φτηνός	αργός	γρήγορος
όμορφος	άσκημος	παράξενος	μακρύς

GAME CARD 6 (see page 63)

Picture cards:

You are here

τέσσερα	ένα	εφτά	εννέα
δέκα	οχτώ	τρία	δύο
οχτώ	έξι	εφτά	ένα
έξι	εννέα	τέσσερα	έξι

δύο	ένα	τρία	δύο
τρία	πέντε	έξι	εφτά
οχτώ	πέντε	δέκα	εννέα
τρία	τέσσερα	εφτά	τρία

1

2

3

4

5

6

7

8

9

10

Picture cards:

Profession cards:

δάσκαλος	λογιστής	γιατρός	οδηγός
ηθοποιός	μάγειρας	υπάλληλος	μάγειρας
φοιτητής			